PREPARE
O BETHLEHEM

Other books published by the Orthodox Research Institute include:

William C. Mills. *From Pascha to Pentecost: Reflections on the Gospel of John*

Saint Cyril of Alexandria. *Against Those Who Are Unwilling to Confess that the Holy Virgin Is Theotokos.* Introduction, Greek Text and English Translation by Protopresbyter George Dion. Dragas

Metropolitan Makarios (Tillyrides) of Kenya and Irinoupolis. *Adventures in the Unseen: The Silent Witness.* Vol. I: Harare, Zimbabwe, 2000

Protopresbyter George Dion. Dragas. *Ecclesiasticus I: Introducing Eastern Orthodoxy*

Protopresbyter George Dion. Dragas. *Ecclesiasticus II: Orthodox Icons, Saints, Feasts and Prayer*

Protopresbyter George Dion. Dragas. *The Lord's Prayer according to Saint Makarios of Corinth*

Protopresbyter George Dion. Dragas. *On the Priesthood and the Holy Eucharist: According to St. Symeon of Thessalonica, Patriarch Kallinikos of Constantinople and St. Mark Eugenikos of Ephesus*

Protopresbyter George Dion. Dragas. *Saint Athanasius of Alexandria: Original Research and New Perspectives*

Protopresbyter George Dion. Dragas. *St. Cyril of Alexandria's Teaching on the Priesthood*

Protopresbyter John S. Romanides. *An Outline of Orthodox Patristic Dogmatics,* in Greek and English. Edited and translated by Protopresbyter George Dion. Dragas

Rev. Dr. Steven Bigham. *Early Christian Attitudes toward Images*

PREPARE
O BETHLEHEM

Reflections on the Scripture Readings
for the Christmas-Epiphany Season

William C. Mills

ORTHODOX
RESEARCH
INSTITUTE
Rollinsford, New Hampshire

Published by Orthodox Research Institute
20 Silver Lane
Rollinsford, NH 03869
www.orthodoxresearchinstitute.org

Cover artwork by Taisia Mills

Library of Congress Control Number: 2005934460

ISBN 1-933275-03-0

Prepare O Bethlehem
For Eden Has Been Opened to All
Adorn Yourself O Ephratha
For the Tree of Life Blossoms Forth from
the Virgin in the Cave
Her Womb Is a Spiritual Paradise
Planted with the Fruit Divine
If Eat of It We Will Live Forever
And Not Die Like Adam
Christ Is Coming To Restore the Image
Which He Made in the Beginning!

— Troparion for the Prefeast of Christmas

In Blessed Memory
Donald and Sonia Mills

and

With Deep Gratitude
Father John and Barbara Ealy

TABLE OF CONTENTS

PRAYER BEFORE THE GOSPEL
(From the Divine Liturgy of Saint John Chrysostom)

Illumine our hearts O master who loves mankind, with the pure light of Thy divine knowledge. Open the eyes of our mind to the understanding of Thy Gospel teachings. Implant also in us the fear of Thy blessed commandments, that, trampling down all carnal desires, we may enter upon a spiritual manner of living, both thinking and doing such things as are well pleasing unto Thee. For Thou art the illumination of our souls and bodies, O Christ our God, and unto Thee we ascribe glory, together with Thy Father, who is from everlasting, and Thine all-holy, good, and life-creating Spirit, now and ever and unto ages of ages. Amen.

INTRODUCTION

The Christmas season is a wonderful time of year. It is a time of gift giving, family gatherings, office parties, school plays, winter vacations, and of course, winter sports: sledding, skating, snowboarding, and skiing. This time of year would not be the same without building snowmen, making gingerbread houses, drinking hot chocolate and caroling around the neighborhood. Christmas always reminds me of cookies baking in the oven and the fresh smell of a newly cut Christmas tree. It is also a hectic time as we venture out into the local malls searching patiently for a parking spot so that we can purchase a perfect gift for our loved one. Christmas is enough to give angst even to the most savvy of shoppers!

Yet, while we are generally preoccupied with planning and attending family gatherings, we also know that in the background we patiently await the celebration of the birth of our Lord and Savior Jesus Christ, the Prince of Peace and the Savior of the World. Sometimes Christmas comes and goes without much thought as we prepare for New Year's parties and then the thought of returning back to work after our holiday vacation. Unfortunately, the "reason for the season" gets lost in the middle of Christmas shopping and end of year related business. *Prepare O Bethlehem* was written so that we can take a few moments out of our busy life and reflect on the Scripture lessons of the Christmas season in order to make this feast a more meaningful time of year.

There are numerous Scripture lessons from both the Old and New Testaments that are prescribed for the Christmas and Epiphany season. Rather than provide a commentary on the Scripture lessons as they appear in the Church lectionary, I chose the New Testament lessons in

Matthew 1–2 and Luke 1–3 as the basis for my reflection. However, the individual reflections include numerous citations and references to the other Scripture readings for Christmas, especially the Old Testament prophecies as well as selections from other parts of the Gospels. The reader is encouraged to read all of the Scripture citations in order to obtain a full understanding of the Gospel message. I have included an appendix in the back of the book which includes the lectionary readings for the Christmas season for anyone who is interested in reading and studying the Scriptures according to their lectionary setting.

In another appendix, I have also included two Christmas sermons, one by St. John Chrysostom and the other by St. Gregory Nazianzus. John and Gregory were devout pastors and bishops in the Church and are known for theological writings which are still read today for insight into how they read and interpreted Scripture. Scripture was the foundation for their theological reflections and was the fabric from which the major doctrines of the Church were formulated. The Church historian Robert Louis Wilken emphasizes the biblical nature of early Christian theology in the following manner:

> Because the words and images of the Bible endure, they provided scaffolding on which to construct the edifice of Christian thought. The Bible was, however, more than a platform on which to build something else, and biblical interpretation was not a stage on a way to the real way of thinking. Thinking took place through exegesis, and the language of the Bible became the language of Christian thought. Christian thinkers returned again and again to a bountiful spring from which, says Ambrose, flow "rivers of understanding, rivers of meditation and spiritual rivers."[1]

My hope is that these sermons provide the foundation for our understanding of the Christmas feast in regards to the rest of the Church year but also in our acceptance of Jesus Christ as the Son of God, which is the main message in this festal celebration. I hope that the reader will turn to the Scriptures as a "river of understanding" as we read the Gospels for Christmas.

---

[1] Robert Louis Wilken, *The Spirit of Early Christian Thought* (New Haven, CT: Yale University Press, 2003).

In the appendix, I also included a selection of liturgical hymns for Epiphany that were composed by the great hymnographer, Ephrem the Syrian. The reader will notice that the rhetorical style is very different than what we encounter in our modern culture. The hymns draw heavily from the Scriptures as he comments on the importance of oil (chrism) in connection with the gift of the Holy Spirit given at Epiphany. Hopefully, these sermons and hymns will provide the reader with further reflection on the importance of the Christmas feast as we welcome God Himself into our midst.

The introduction is organized in two parts. Part one provides an overview of the Christmas and Epiphany season according to the Orthodox liturgical tradition. The liturgical setting for the Scripture readings will provide a context for reading and reflecting on the prescribed Scripture lessons. Part two is an overview on the importance of both personal and small group Bible study as a vital area within a parish community. My hope is that *Prepare O Bethlehem* can be used for small group Bible study in the parish.

Part One: The Season of Christmas. According to the Orthodox Church calendar, the official name for Christmas is: The Nativity according to the Flesh of Our Lord God and Savior Jesus Christ, or sometimes referred to as simply the Nativity.[2] I will refer to it as Christmas for short. In addition to the celebration of Christmas on December 25, the Christmas season includes also the Circumcision and Naming of Jesus on January 1; the Baptism in the Jordan River, called the Epiphany or Theophany, on January 6; and the Entrance of the Lord into the Temple on February 2. These three feasts celebrate the gift of the Word of God who is fully revealed to us in the person of Jesus Christ. These feasts also reveal to us God's saving work in the world through His Son. It is tempt-

---

[2] There are several good overviews on the liturgical and theological meaning of the Christmas and Epiphany season, see especially, Thomas Hopko, *The Winter Pascha* (Crestwood, NY: St. Vladimir's Seminary Press, 1984); Thomas J. Talley, *The Origins of the Liturgical Year* (Collegeville, MN: The Liturgical Press, 1986); Olga Dunlop (translator), *Living God: A Catechism Volume 1* (Crestwood, NY: St. Vladimir's Seminary Press, 1996); and Department of Religious Education, *The Services of Christmas: The Nativity of our Lord God and Savior Jesus Christ* (Syosset, NY: Orthodox Church in America, 1981).

ing to see these three feasts as mere historical events in the life of Jesus which some scholars have done in the past.[3] However, if we carefully listen to the liturgical hymnography of the Church, we see that while these events are recorded in the Gospel narratives, they are also presented to us today as yet another example of the Gospel of salvation. While Jesus did die 2,000 years ago, He is very much alive in the world through the proclamation of the Gospel. Thus, Jesus is still alive and present for us today. Hence, the word "today" is often repeated in the hymns as a reminder of God's present saving action in our lives:

Today heaven and earth are united for Christ is born
Today God has come to earth and man ascends to heaven
Today, God who by nature cannot be seen,
Is seen in the flesh for our sake.
Let us glorify Him, crying:
Glory to God in the highest, and on earth peace!
Thy coming has brought peace to us:
Glory to Thee, our Savior!
　　　　　— *Stikhera on the Litya Great Compline for Christmas*

Today You have shone forth in our world, O Lord
And the light of Your countenance has been marked on us
Knowing You we sing Your praises
You have come and revealed Yourself
O unapproachable light.
　　　　　— *Kontakion of the Feast of Epiphany*

Today Symeon the elder enters the temple rejoicing in spirit,
To receive in his arms Him who gave the law to Moses
He who himself now fulfills the law
For Moses was counted worthy to see God through darkness
　　and sounds not clear.
And his face covered he rebuked the unbelieving hearts of
　　the Hebrews
But Symeon carried the Pre-Eternal Word of the Father in
　　bodily form,
And he revealed the Light of the Gentiles, the Cross and
　　the Resurrection.
Anna was proved to be a prophetess, preaching the Savior
　　and Deliverer of Israel

---

[3] See Luke Timothy Johnson, *The Real Jesus* (N.Y.: Harper Collins, 1998) and *Living Jesus* (N.Y.: Harper Collins, 1999).

> Unto Him let us cry aloud O Christ our God, through the
> prayers of the Theotokos have mercy on us.
> — *Stikhera on the Litya Feast of the Meeting of*
> *our Lord and Savior in the Temple*

These hymns remind us that while Jesus Christ has already come in the flesh and was crucified for us and for our salvation, He also comes again as a child in the manger and in the Temple and as an adult in the River Jordan as a reminder of the great gift of our redemption and salvation. Today, we are saved through our faith in Him, and today, we rejoice in His baptism in the River Jordan. The repetition of "today" is quite meaningful as we ponder the saving mysteries of God in His Son Jesus. We also know that even though He already came as an infant, He will also come again as the judge in order to bring God's justice to the world. Thus, we need to be vigilant because we know neither the time nor the place nor the hour of his coming:

> But of that day or that hour no one knows, not even the angels in heaven, nor the Son, but only the Father. Take heed, watch, for you do not know when the time will come. It is like a man going on a journey, when he leaves home and puts his servants in charge, each with his work, and commands the doorkeeper to be on watch. Watch, therefore, for you do not know when the master of the house will come, in the evening, or at midnight, or at cockcrow, or in the morning — lest he come suddenly and find you asleep. And what I say to you I say to all: Watch (Mark 13:32–37. See also Acts 1:7).

However, while we await His coming again, we also ponder the great mystery of His birth in the flesh. Jesus' birth is one of the most solemn feasts of the Church but which is also filled with great joy.

The word joy and rejoice are found throughout the birth narratives. The Gospel of Matthew tells us that when the magi encountered the star they "rejoiced exceedingly with great joy" (Matthew 2:10). When Mary visited Elizabeth and told her that she was with child, Luke says that the babe in Elizabeth's womb "leaped for joy" (Luke 1:44). The babe was John who was later called the Baptist. When the angel came to the shepherds to announce the good news of the birth of Jesus, they brought "news of great joy" (Luke 2:10).

As with all liturgical seasons, we go through a time of preparation and anticipation for the feast; Pascha, or Easter is preceeded by Great Lent, the Dormition or Falling Asleep of the Theotokos is preceeded by the Dormition Fast, and Christmas is preceeded by a Lenten period called Advent. Advent begins on November 15 and concludes at the Divine Liturgy on Christmas day.

Advent is derived from the Latin word "advenire," which means to come. During Advent, we prepare for the coming of the Lord. Our preparations include participating in the liturgical services of the Church, especially participating in the sacrament of holy confession and holy communion, increasing our almsgiving to the poor and needy, and reading the Scripture on a regular basis.

Unlike Great Lent, Advent does not begin with a special liturgical service and does not have a Rite of Forgiveness or include special Lenten melodies. There are no special services such as the Liturgy of the Presanctified Gifts or Memorial Saturdays. However, the Church is decked in either crimson or maroon liturgical vestments as a reminder that we are in a Lenten season. Instead, we are gradually introduced to the feast throughout the forty-day Advent season.

The first mention of the birth of Christ is on the eve of the Feast of the Entrance of the Theotokos into the Temple on November 21. In this service, we hear for the first time the Christmas canon with the words: *Christ is Born! Glorify Him!* The canon is sung during the weeks leading up to Christmas:

> Christ is born: glorify Him!
> Christ comes from heaven; go to meet Him!
> Christ is on earth, be exalted!
> Sing to the Lord, all the earth!
> And praise Him in gladness, O people,
> For He has been glorified.

> To the Son, begotten from the Father, before all ages
> And incarnate of the virgin without seed in these latter days
> To Christ our God, let us cry out:
> Though He has raised up our horn
> Holy are Thou, O Lord!

> Stem and flower of the root of Jesse
> Thou has blossomed from the virgin, O Christ.

From the mountain overshadowed by the forest Thou art come,
Made flesh from her that knew no man.
O God, not formed from matter
Glory to Thy power, O Lord!

O God of Peace, Father of mercies,
Thou has sent Thine angel of great counsel to grant us peace.
We are guided to the light of the knowledge of God,
And keeping watch by the night,
We glorify Thee, O lover of Man!

The sea monster cast forth Jonah as it had received him,
Like a babe from the womb.
And when the Word came to dwell in the virgin and was made flesh,
He came forth preserving her uncorrupt,
For as he himself was not subject to decay,
He kept his mother free from harm.

The children brought up together in godliness
Scorned the impious decree of the tyrant
They were not afraid of the threat of fire
But standing in the midst of the flames they sang:
Blessed art Thou O God of our fathers!

The furnace moist with dew
Was an image prefiguring a wonder beyond nature,
For it did not burn the children whom it had received
Nor did the fire of Divinity consume the virgin's womb when it
      entered it
So let us raise the song:
Let all creation bless the Lord
And exalt him throughout all ages!

Magnify, O my soul
The most pure virgin Theotokos
More honorable and more glorious than the heavenly hosts.

The Christmas canon is a beautiful hymn based on a sermon by
the fourth century pastor and theologian St. Gregory Nazianzus.[4]
Gregory bases his sermon the Old Testament prophecies of Jesus'
birth especially the prophecy from Isaiah concerning the root of Jesse
as the source from which the messiah will come. Gregory, also draws
upon the story of Daniel and the three youths, Shadrach, Meshach and

---

[4]Gregory, together with Basil of Caesarea and John Chrysostom, are the three great
hierarchs in the Orthodox Church. They are commemorated together on January 30.

Abednego, who were thrown into the firery furnace at the request of King Nebuchednezzar. The youths were unharmed in the midst of the great fire. Gregory likens the children in the firey furnace with the virginal birth; while Mary contained the fire of God Himself she was not burned up or consumed by it, a theme which reoccurs in the liturgical hymnography for Christmas.

Then, we next hear these words about the birth of Jesus on the Vespers of St. Andrew of Crete celebrated on November 28:

> Rejoice, O Isaiah, and receive the Word of God.
> Prophesy to Mary the Maiden
> She is the burning bush consumed by the fire of divinity
> Adorn yourself, O Bethlehem
> Open your gates, O Eden.
> Enter, O magi, and see the babe swaddled in a crib.
> Behold the star shining above the cave
>
> Tell us, O Joseph, how you led the Virgin
> Into the Bethlehem cave
> "After searching the Scriptures and hearing the angel," he says,
> I am certain that Mary will wondrously give birth to God
> Whom the wise men from the East will worship
> Offering to Him their precious gifts"
> O Lord, incarnate for our sake, glory to You.
> — *Verses on "Lord I Call" Feast of St. Andrew*

The hymnography for the feast of St. Andrew provides us with more detail concerning the birth narrative, we hear about Bethlehem, Joseph, Mary and the visitation of the Magi. Likewise, the hymns speak of the role of the Virgin Mary in the birth story, that she is the burning bush that is not consumed, echoing a beautiful passage in Exodus 3 where Moses encounters God Himself in the burning bush on Mt. Sinai. The bush burns but is not consumed. Thus, Mary is described as the burning bush which contained the powerful Word of God but was not consumed by it which also echoes the theme of Daniel and the three youths in the furnace.

Beginning in the month of December, the Church remembers many of the prophets of the Old Testament: Nahum (December 1), Habakkuk (December 2), Zephaniah (December 3), Haggai (December 16), and Daniel and the Three Youths (December 17).

While there are no special services prescribed for these saints' days, their inclusion in the Church calendar reminds us of the prophetic promise of the messiah, that God does not forget His people. The lectionary includes many readings from the prophets for the three feasts of Christmas, Epiphany and the Entrance into the Temple. The prophets foretell not only of the coming of the messiah, but also of our sin, of our need for repentance, and of God's everlasting love towards his people which is expressed in terms of divine justice and righteousness. These themes recur throughout the lectionary readings during the Christmas season.[5]

Then, the next time we hear about the birth of Jesus is during Vespers for the feast of St. Nicholas, Archbishop of Myra in Lycia, on December 6. We hear this hymn about the birth of Christ:

> Make ready, O cave, for the Mother-Lamb comes
> Bearing Christ in her womb
> Recieve Him, O manger, who by a word released the dwellers on
>   earth from all lawlessness.
> You shepherds abiding in the fields,
> Bear witness to the awesome wonder.
> — *Verses on "Lord I Call" Feast of St. Nicholas*

The popular and cultural portrait of St. Nicholas has reduced a humble and dedicated pastor into a gift giver without any reference to his Christian roots. However, the real St. Nicholas was a dedicated and devoted pastor to his flock, especially to the women and children. He cared for the poor and the homeless, and provided material assistance whenever possible. St. Nicholas is a reminder during this Advent season that Godly love is incarnated in both our words and actions, especially in our charitable giving to the poor and needy of our communities.

The two Sundays before Christmas are dedicated to the faithful Forefathers and holy men and women who came before Jesus. The epistle reading for the Sunday before Christmas is from the letter to the Hebrews.

---

[5] I have included numerous passages from the prophetic books to show the intimate connection and continuity between the Old and New Testaments. The reader is invited to read these prophetic books in their entirety because they are the fabric from which the New Testament was woven. The prophets also provide us with language, images and symbols which are repeated throughout the New Testament literature.

In this long passage, we hear of many faithful men and women who prepared the way for Jesus (Hebrews 11:9–10, 17–23, 32–40). I have included a larger portion of the text in order to see the full message of the author:

> By faith Abel offered to God a more acceptable sacrifice than Cain, through which he received approval as righteousness, God bearing witness by accepting his gifts; he died, but through his faith he is still speaking. By faith Enoch was taken up so that he should not see death; and he was not found, because God had taken him. Now before he was taken he was attested as having pleased God. And without faith it is impossible to please him. For whoever would draw near to God must believe that He exists and that He rewards those who seek Him. By faith Noah, being warned by God concerning events as yet unseen, took heed and constructed an ark for the saving of his household; by the righteousness which comes by faith. By faith Abraham obeyed when he was called to go out to a place which he was to receive as an inheritance and went out not knowing where he was to go. By faith he sojourned in the land of promise, as in a foreign land, living in tents with Isaac and Jacob, heirs with him of the same promise. For he looked forward to the city which has foundations, whose builder and maker is God. By faith Sarah herself received power to conceive, even when she was past the age, since she considered him faithful had promised … by faith Abraham, when he was tested offered up Isaac, and he who had received the promises was ready to offer up his only son, of whom it was said, "Through Isaac shall your descendants be named." He considered that God was able to raise men even from the dead; hence figuratively speaking, he did receive him back. By faith Isaac invoked future blessings on Jacob and Esau. By faith Jacob, when dying, blessed each of the sons of Joseph, bowing in worship over the head of his staff. By faith Joseph, at the end of his life; made mention of the exodus of the Israelites and gave directions concerning his burial (Hebrews 11:4–11, 17–22).

The text continues as the author speaks of the faithfulness of Moses, David, Gideon, Barak, Samuel and the prophets. We remember their obedience to the word of God and their perseverance in the face of evil as we prepare to receive the ultimate Word of God in our midst. Although they all died before Christ was born, they all lived in anticipation and hopefulness that God would redeem His people and bring salvation to the earth. Thus, at Christmas time, we remember their faithfulness as we too try to be faithful to God in our life. It was their faith in God which led them to obedience and perseverance, two qualities which are emphasized throughout the readings for Christmas.

Then, beginning on December 19, the Orthodox Church begins celebrating the Prefeast services. These services are a combination of Vespers with Compline. While no special Scripture readings are prescribed, the liturgical hymnography draws our attention to the preparation for the birth of Jesus. These hymns are scriptural reflections on the birth narratives, telling us about the star in the East, the virgin birth, the shepherds, the magi and the flight into Egypt. Likewise, each evening we hear the Prefeast troparion from which the title of this book is taken:

Prepare O Bethlehem
For Eden has been opened to all
Adorn yourself, O Ephratha
For the Tree of Life blossoms forth from the Virgin in the cave
Her womb is a spiritual paradise
Planted with the fruit divine
If eat of it we will live forever
And not die like Adam
Christ is coming to restore the image which He made in the beginning!
— *Troparion for the Prefeast*

Each evening, the hymns of the Prefeast services draw our attention to the "reason for the season." We recall that the birth of Christ is a joyful event, but at the same time, we recall that this Christ was born in order to die. We face the reality that while the light has come into the world, the world prefers the darkness to light. Some of the hymns of the Prefeast services are patterned after the ones for Pascha and echo the Paschal themes:

Holy Week — Holy Thursday Matins	Nativity — Troparion Ninth Hour of the Royal Hours of Christmas
Today He who hung the earth upon the waters is hung upon the tree. He who wraps the heavens in a cloud is wrapped in the purple of mockery. He who freed Adam in the Jordan is slapped in the face. The bridegroom of the Church is affixed to the cross with nails We worship Thy passion O Christ (Three times)	Today He who holds the whole creation in His hand is born of a virgin. God who in the beginning fashioned the heavens lies in a manger. He who rained manna on His people in the wilderness is fed on milk from His mother's breasts. The bridegroom of the Church summons the wise men. The son of the virgin accepts their gifts.

Show us also Thy glorious resurrection.	We worship Thy Nativity O Christ (Three times) Show us also Thy glorious Theophany.

These hymns are very similar in that they are based on similar biblical themes. The one from the Nativity highlights God's power through His Son Jesus, who is the fulfillment of the Old Testament. The hymn from Holy Week emphasizes the fact that at the end of His life Jesus was ultimately weak, the one who was beaten and afflicted for our salvation. But at the passion, we also look forward to the glorious resurrection of Christ which we celebrate on Pascha. Likewise, the hymn from Christmas also looks forward to the feast of Epiphany, since at Epiphany, we celebrate the preaching of the Gospel, which is the beginning of Jesus' public ministry.

The Christmas celebration begins in a very solemn manner with the service of Royal Hours which is very similar to the Royal Hours for Holy Friday. Royal Hours consist of Gospel readings that are interspersed with the singing of troparia and other hymns. Following Royal Hours, the Church celebrates the Vesperal Divine Liturgy of St. Basil the Great, which includes numerous Old Testament readings. Following the Liturgy, we begin the All Night Vigil which includes Great Compline and Matins. Here, we begin to announce the great news that "Christ is Born" and the response "Glorify Him!" We use this greeting during the week following Christmas as we continue the celebration of the feast. Then, on the feast itself, we celebrate the Divine Liturgy of St. John Chrysostom followed by the breaking of the fast as we share the joy and warmth of the holidays.[6]

The feast of Christmas continues for five more days as we remember the most holy Theotokos on December 26, the first martyr Stephen on December 27, and then the holy innocents killed in Bethlehem on December 29. Then, we encounter the feast of the Circumcision and Naming of Jesus on January 1, which then leads us to the Prefeast services of Epiphany.[7]

---

[6] The services for Christmas and Epiphany are rather complex. Liturgical details for these feasts can be found in the typikon.

[7] The feast of the Circumcision and Naming of Jesus does not have prescribed Prefeast services.

Epiphany, also called Theophany, has a series of five-day Prefeast services which parallel the Prefeast services for Christmas. We first prepare ourselves for the birth of the Word of God in the flesh, and then we prepare or anticipate the public announcement or manifestation of Jesus to the world in the feast of Theophany or Epiphany. The word Theophany comes from the Greek and means "manifestation." While at Christmas we celebrate the birth of the messiah, at Epiphany we celebrate the beginning of his proclamation of the Kingdom:

> The Feast of Christ's birth has passed;
> It shone more brightly than the sun.
> The day of His epiphany is coming;
> That day will be even more radiant.
> There the shepherds gave glory with the angels,
> Worshipping God made man.
> Here John's right hand will touch the master,
> As he cries out in fear;
> Sanctify both me and the waters,
> O only merciful one.
>
> The feast which passed was radiant,
> But the coming one is even more glorious!
> There the magi worshipped the savior:
> Here the servant baptizes the master.
> Here the shepherds saw the child and were amazed;
> Here the voice of the Father proclaims the only-begotten Son!
>
> Come O Faithful,
> Let us celebrate the prefeast of Christ's theophany!
> Let us sing hymns to honor the noble baptism of our God.
> For He wills to approach the forerunner in the flesh.
> As a man He asks for the baptism of salvation:
> The regeneration of all those who accept Him in faith
> And become partakers of the spirit!

These hymns emphasize that while the birth of Jesus is important, His baptism which is the beginning of His public ministry, is even more important, "The feast which passed was radiant, but the coming one is even more glorious!"

During the feast of Epiphany, the priest blesses water to commemorate the baptism in the Jordan, and to remind us that God continually blesses and sanctifies us through material things such as bread, wine, oil, fruit, flowers and water. We also have home blessings during the Epiphany season. The priest visits and blesses our homes with the holy water that was blessed at the feast of Epiphany. The troparion for the Epiphany season reminds us of our salvation through the baptismal waters of Jesus:

> When Thou O Lord was baptized in the Jordan
> The worship of the Trinity was made manifest
> For the voice of the Father bore witness to Thee
> And called Thee His beloved Son
> And the Spirit in the form of a dove
> Confirmed the truthfulness of His word
> O Christ Our God who has revealed Thyself
> And has enlightened the world glory to Thee.
>
> *— Troparion for Epiphany*

Finally, the Christmas season culminates with the celebration of the feast of the Entrance of the Lord into the Temple, which is also known as the Meeting of the Lord. This is celebrated on February 2, forty days after Christmas, and completes the Christmas season. While no special Prefeast services are prescribed, we celebrate this feast in the usual manner with either Great Vespers or the Vigil and the Divine Liturgy:

> Adorn your bridal chamber, O Zion, and welcome Christ the King
> Salute Mary the heavenly gate
> For she has been made as a throne of the Cherubim
> And she carries the king of glory
> A cloud of light is the Virgin
> Who has born in the flesh the Son begotten before the morning star
> Symeon taking Him in the arms, proclaimed to the people
> This is the Lord of life and death and the Savior of the world.

> The mother who has never known wedlock has brought into the temple
> Him who shone forth before the ages from the Father
> He who in latter times was born form a virgin's womb
> He who gave the law on Mount Sinai
> Makes Himself obedient to the ordinances of the law
> And she who brought Him to the priest and righteous elder
> Whose appointed lot it was to see Christ the Lord
> Symeon, receiving Him in his arms, greatly rejoiced, crying aloud
> This is God, coeternal with the Father, and the deliverer of our souls.

> The Theotokos, Mary, carried in her arms
> Him who is borne aloft upon the chariot of the Cherubim

He is praised in song by the Seraphim
And was flesh of her without knowing wedlock
She gave into the arms of the priest and elder
The giver of the law who fulfills the commandment of the law
Holding the Life he asked to be released from life saying
Now, O master let me depart to declare to Adam
That I have seen the pre-eternal God and Savior of the world
Who was made a babe without undergoing change.

> — *Aposticha Feast of the Meeting of our Lord and
> Savior Jesus Christ in the Temple*

Because we are usually so busy and preoccupied with so many things during the holiday season, these three feasts sometimes take a back seat to other holiday activities. Sometimes, we have to make difficult choices in life, and very often, Church may not always be high on our list. This is unfortunate, because these winter feasts are so meaningful, especially when we are familiar with the Gospel lessons from these festal celebrations. Hopefully, during the Christmas season, we shall return to the Scriptures so we can know the truth, which is Christ Himself, "Jesus said to the Jews who had believed in him, 'If you continue in My word, you are truly My disciples, and you will know the truth and the truth will make you free'" (John 8:31). The Scriptures are the source for our knowledge of the biblical God, His Son Jesus Christ and the life-giving Spirit. *Prepare O Bethlehem* will invite you to return to the Word of God, which leads us to know the Word who became flesh for us and for our salvation. Thus, *Prepare O Bethlehem* can serve as the basis for both a personal or group Bible study. Below, I have provided some guidance as to establishing and sustaining a vibrant Bible study in the parish. If you do not have a regular Bible study program in your parish, please consult your priest to begin one. A regular Bible study will foster and cultivate formation in the faith and provide a wonderful opportunity for parishioners to share fellowship with one another.

P ART TWO. BIBLE STUDY IN THE PARISH. Regular Bible study is a necessary and vital part of parish life. A vibrant Bible study program will not only cultivate long-time friendships and fellowship among parishioners, but it will encourage us to read and learn the Word of God so that we may better understand the biblical God, and live according to His commandments. Likewise, when we participate in Bible study, whether as individuals or in a group, we begin to realize that our liturgical services are either directly or indirectly based on the Scriptures! All of the liturgical hymns, prayers and services include numerous scriptural references and quotations. If we follow the liturgical texts carefully, we realize that the services direct our minds toward God's Word. So, the more we study Scripture on our own, the more connections we make between what we read and what we hear in the liturgical services.

Today, more than ever, we need to foster Scripture study in our Church school programs, adult education classes and catechumen classes so that this generation of Orthodox Christians knows the Word of God, not only for its own sake, but more importantly, for the true knowledge of God which the Gospel of John says is eternal life. A thorough understanding of God's Word is the foundation for preaching, teaching, catechesis, evangelism, Church growth and educational programs. Likewise, our Creed and doctrines are also based on the Word of God. The simple fact is that we have to learn Scripture — it is the foundation of our Christian faith.

It is tempting to quickly read a passage in the Bible and then move on to the rest of our daily activities. However, much is lost if we quickly read the Bible. We often miss the entire point of the lesson if we read too fast. The reader is encouraged to take ample time and slowly read each passage, think about what you are reading, and then continue. This method is called *lectio divina*, or divine reading, and has been practiced by Christians in both East and West for centuries. *Lectio divina*, or simply called *lectio*, is a slow, meditative way of reading Scripture by which the reader ruminates or actually "chews" on each word, considers what the word means and how it connects to the rest of Scripture. It takes time to reflect on the Scripture lesson and *lectio* cannot be rushed.

Practicing *lectio* will force us to slowly and critically read through the Scriptures so that we will be more open to reading and hearing the Word of God as it is written. As many ancients have attested, *lectio* will open your mind to a new way of reading the Word of God, one that will hopefully be a life-long process. I have included a few resources in the bibliography about how to practice *lectio.*

Prepare O Bethlehem can be used as a resource when practicing *lectio divina*. Read the daily Gospel lesson slowly and carefully. Then, after reading the Gospel lesson a few times, read the reflection in *Prepare O Bethlehem*. Consider the various words or phrases that are emphasized or discussed in the reflection. You are also encouraged to look up the Biblical references from both the Old and New Testaments which are included with each reflection. These references show the intimate connection between each Gospel reading and the rest of the Scriptures. After reading the reflection, re-read the Gospel in light of what was discussed in the commentary.

However, one of the most important reasons for practicing *lectio* is to hear God speaking to us today! While the Scriptures were written over 2,000 years ago, they are meant to be applied in our life, in our particular sitaution, and specific circumstances. *Lectio* will open hearts and minds to hearing the good news for us now. Hopefully, we will, with much humility, begin to obey this word as it takes shape in our heart:

> Commit yourself to putting God's word into action, so you will not be condemned by the One who will judge us. Judgment will be based on not how much we have heard, but on how well we have put what we have heard into practice in our lives-in the personal, social, professional, political and ecclesiastical dimensions of our lives. After we listen, the task left to us is to believe and to let our faith bear the fruit of the spirit, "love, joy, peace, patience, good will, kindness, faithfulness, humility, self-control" (Galatians 5:22). Thus we will come to experience the great joy of God's merciful love.[8]

SMALL GROUP BIBLE STUDY. *Prepare O Bethlehem* can also be used as a resource in a small group Bible study, especially during the Christmas season. A parish Bible study program is an excellent way to read and study the Scriptures within a community of other Orthodox Christians. Bible studies also provide wonderful opportunities to share in Christian fellowship and may serve as an outreach ministry to the local community.

There are many ways to conduct a Bible study. One of the most common ways is a lectionary study where the epistle and Gospel readings

---

[8] Enzo Bianchi, *Praying the Word: An Introduction to Lectio Divina* (Kalamazoo, IN: Cistercian Publications, 1998), p. 81.

for the following Sunday are read and studied. This allows the participants to prepare themselves to hear the Scripture during the following
Divine Liturgy and also to prepare to hear the sermon, since the sermon
generally follows the Scripture readings for the day.

Another way to study the Scriptures is a word study. In this format,
a word or set of words are used as the context for the Bible study. Here,
the leader chooses certain words such as love, neighbor or justice, and
by using a concordance, he or she will select passages from the Bible using this word. This method allows the group to read a larger portion of
the Bible and to focus on a select number of words in order to better understand their meaning. For example, the group can focus on the word
"love" in the Gospel of Matthew or the word "love" as the Apostle Paul
uses it in his letters. This method of study might be useful to groups that
do not meet very often or do not have a fixed number of participants
each week.

Finally, one of the best ways to study the Scripture is to select an
entire book such as the Gospel of Luke and follow it chapter by chapter
each week. This method is good for several reasons. Firstly, its focus on
one book of the Bible allows the group to better understand the words
and meaning of that book. Secondly, it follows this book throughout the
course of one year or part of a year, taking one chapter per week. The participants may encounter some of the readings during the Divine Liturgy
as well, which will reinforce what they learned at the Bible study.

It is important that one person serves as the group leader. The leader's task is to be prepared to discuss the selected Gospel lesson in some
detail, and thus, *Prepare O Bethlehem* can serve as an additional resource
for this purpose. At the beginning of each Bible study, the participants
are encouraged to read the Gospel lesson out loud so that everyone
hears the Scripture together. Then, the leader can highlight specific
words, expressions or themes in the lesson, using *Prepare O Bethlehem*
when appropriate. A portion of time should be allotted for group discus-
sion and common reflection on the lesson. The Bible study should open
and close with prayer.

RESOURCES FOR BIBLE STUDY. Many people begin reading Scripture and become frustrated, bored or lost in the vast amount of information contained in the Bible. Words or phrases may seem unfamiliar; terms and concepts might seem foreign; and many names and geographical places seem far removed from our cultural understanding. Likewise, we may be confused as we thumb through numerous translations of the Bible, trying to find the one that we find conducive to Bible study. This may end up in what is generally called DBS or the "dusty Bible syndrome" — everyone has a Bible, but never reads it! There are many resources that may assist in reading and studying the Scriptures. Resources such as those listed in the bibliography can help in comprehending key concepts and words.

It is important to have access to a translation of the Bible that you feel comfortable reading. There are numerous translations available. I like to use the Revised Standard Version (RSV), but there are other ones that are also conducive to Bible study such as the Jerome Bible (JB), New International Version (NIV), or the King James or New King James Versions (KJV or NKJV). It is helpful to have more than one translation available so you can compare words and phrases from each text. Likewise, many Bibles are called "study Bibles," which means that they contain copious notes and cross-references for further reading and reflection. It is important to look up the various cross-references in the Scripture reading so you are familiar with similar passages in the Bible.

One of the most important reference tools is a concordance. A concordance contains a complete list of all of the words in the Bible and the specific chapters and verses where you can locate them. For example, if you look up the word "salvation" in a concordance, it will direct you to every single verse where the term salvation is used. Similarly, a Bible dictionary provides concise definitions of proper names, geographical place names and definitions of weights, measures and social and cultural concepts. A Bible dictionary also provides background information on the formation of the Scriptures and historical information about the various Bible translations.

Finally, a serious student of the Scriptures should have a Bible commentary handy because a commentary will provide the detailed discussions of Biblical words and phrases. Smaller commentaries may be devoted to a single book of the Bible, such as Genesis or Luke, and larger commentaries cover the entire Bible. Other resources such as Bible maps, atlases and lexicons also can assist you in your life-long study of Scripture.

A word of thanks is owed to four important people who helped make this book possible. First and foremost, I am eternally grateful for the editorial skill of Elizabeth Green who always keeps me humble during the editorial process. Her critical eye and sense of style has taught me a great deal as a writer and which I am ever so grateful. Likewise, I am always inspired by the everlasting patience, love and generosity of my beloved wife Taisia and daughter Hannah who sacrificed precious time away from their husband and daddy so he could finish this book. A word of thanksgiving is due to my longtime friend Ann Zinzel who always inspires me to write for the building up of the Body of Christ — alleluia!.

Christ is Born! Glorify Him!

CHAPTER ONE

ELIZABETH AND ZECHARIAH

LUKE 1:5–38; 57–80

> The memory of Your prophets Zechariah
> and Elizabeth
> We celebrate today, O Lord
> By their prayers, we beseech You
> Christ God save our souls!
> — *Troparion for the Feast of*
> *Elizabeth and Zechariah*

Unlike Matthew, who begins his Gospel with the birth of Jesus, Luke begins with the birth of John the Baptist, the "voice of one crying in the desert" who comes to prepare the way of the Lord. John is a prominent figure in all four Gospels. He is described as being a prophet who calls people to repentance. We do not know anything about his childhood or youth, Luke only tells us that his parents were Elizabeth and Zechariah. We remember Elizabeth and Zechariah on September 9.

We are told that Zechariah was married to Elizabeth, who was a daughter of Aaron. This small but important piece of information tells us that she was from the lineage of Aaron, who was from the tribe of Levi.[1] Levi was one of the twelve sons of Jacob and was known as the leader of the priestly tribe in Israel:

> The Levitical priests, that is, all the tribe of Levi, shall have no portion or inheritance with Israel; they shall eat the offerings by fire to the Lord, and His rightful dues. They shall have no inheritance among the brethren; the Lord is their inheritance, as He promised them. And this

---

[1] The Levites were also in charge of the Temple in Jerusalem. They are not mentioned too often in the New Testament, but a Levite is mentioned in the parable of the Good Samaritan (Luke 10:29–37).

shall be the priests due from the people, from the offering a sacrifice, whether it be an ox or sheep: they shall give to the priest the shoulder and the two cheeks and the stomach. The first fruits of your grain, of your wine, and of your oil, and the first of the fleece of your sheep, you shall give Him. For the Lord your God has chosen him out of all your tribes, to stand and minister in the name of the Lord, him and his sons for ever" (Deuteronomy 18:1–5. See also Deuteronomy 21:5, 24:8, 2 Samuel 15:24).

Likewise, both Elizabeth and Zechariah were said to be righteous before God, walking in the commandments, and blameless (Luke 1:6). Furthermore, this birth would be a true miracle, since Elizabeth, like Sarah, Rebecca, Rachel and Hannah, was well beyond her childbearing years. Thus, specifically in the story of Abraham and Sarah:

> They said to him, "Where is Sarah your wife?" And he said, "She is in the tent." The Lord said, "I will surely return to you in the spring, and Sarah your wife shall have a son." And Sarah was listening at the tent door behind him. Now Abraham and Sarah were old, advanced in age; it had ceased to be with Sarah after the manner of women. "After I have grown old, and my husband is old, shall I have pleasure? The Lord said to Abraham, "Why did Sarah laugh, and say, 'Shall I indeed bear a child, now that I am old?' Is anything too hard for the Lord? At the appointed time I will return to you, in the spring, and Sarah shall have a son." But Sarah denied saying, "I did not laugh"; for she was afraid. He said, "No, but you did laugh" (Genesis 18:9–15. See also Genesis 16:1–14; 25:21; 30:1, Judges 13:2).

As an angel came to Abraham and Sarah foretelling that Sarah would bear a son, so too, an angel came and told Zechariah that his wife Elizabeth would bear him a son. The angel's name is Gabriel, the same Gabriel that comes to Mary later in the same Gospel. However, unlike Mary's acceptance of the glad tidings, Zechariah doubts the truthfulness of the message, and as a result, Zechariah is struck dumb (Luke 1:18ff). Later, after the birth of his son, Zechariah's mouth was opened, and he gave thanks and offered this prayer to God:

> Blessed be the Lord God of Israel, for He has visited and redeemed His people, and has raised up a horn of salvation for us in the house of His servant David, as He spoke by the mouth of His holy prophets from of old, that we should be saved from our enemies, and from the hand of all who hate us; to perform mercy promised to our fathers, and to remember His holy covenant, the oath which He swore to our

father Abraham, to grant us that we, being delivered from the hand of our enemies, might serve without fear, in holiness and righteousness before Him all the days of our life. And you, child, shall be called the prophet of the Most High; for you will go before the Lord to prepare His ways, to give knowledge of salvation to His people in the forgiveness of their sins, through the tender mercy of our God, when the day shall dawn upon us from on high to give light to those who sit in darkness and shadow of death, to guide our feet into the way of peace" (Luke 1:68–79).

Zechariah's prayer opens with a traditional Jewish way of prayer by blessing God for everything that He has bestowed upon Israel. Likewise, the reference to the horn is a reference to God's saving power. The horn was an ancient symbol of power and authority, especially during times of war or distress (Jeremiah 48:25). Zechariah also mentions great leaders in Israel, such as King David and the first patriarch Abraham together with the prophets of old. God used these people in order to bring His saving peace to His chosen people just as He uses Elizabeth to give birth to John, who will later become the Baptist, and Mary, who gave birth to Jesus.

The birth of John was certainly miraculous, something that neither Zechariah or Elizabeth expected. But, as with Abraham and Sarah, God works in mysterious ways, catches people off guard and tests their faith in the process. The Gospels reveal that nothing is beyond God's power. John is the voice crying in the desert preparing the way for the Christ, and it is he who also will "guide our feet into the way of peace." The preparation of the birth of Jesus begins with the birth of John, and he is truly the forerunner, the one who came before Jesus to prepare the way for our salvation.

CHAPTER TWO

MARY

LUKE 1:46–56

Today the virgin comes to the cave
Where she will give birth to the eternal Word
Hear the glad tidings and rejoice, O universe!
With the angels and shepherds glorify Him
who reveals Himself:
The eternal God, a little child!
— *Kontakion for the Royal Hours of Christmas*

Mary has been a subject for poets, artists, sculptors, writers and theologians. In many museums, one can find her portrait or statue alongside many other famous men and women. Songs and hymns have been dedicated in her honor, and churches, seminaries, monasteries and shrines have been erected in her memory. Many Western Christians have flocked to her shrines at Lourdes, Guadaloupe and Chestehova, and many in the East have venerated her wonderworking icons in Kiev, Sitka, Smolensk and Vladimir. Miracles have been ascribed to her intercessions, and special services and prayers are written for her. She is known as the Queen of Heaven, the Mediatrix and, most importantly, the Theotokos. Liturgical hymns speak of her as the flower that bore the fruit, the golden censor, the New Jerusalem, the ewe that bore the lamb, and her womb is said to be more spacious than the heavens. She is said to be more honorable than the Cherubim and more glorious beyond compare than the Seraphim. Her memory is invoked at every liturgical service as the deacon or priest prays, "Commemorating our most holy, most pure, most blessed and glorious Lady Theotokos and ever-virgin Mary with all the saints, let us commend ourselves and each other, and all our life unto Christ our God." Mary is certainly very special to Christians and will always be remembered for being the mother of our Lord and Savior Jesus Christ. During the Christmas season she is officially commemorated on December 26, which is called the Synaxis of the Theotokos.

It is ironic, however, that while Mary is very prominent in the birth narratives, she is only mentioned a few times in the entire New Testament. While her name is never specifically mentioned, she intervened at the first miracle that Jesus performed in Cana of Galilee where Jesus changed water into wine, "When the wine gave out, the mother of Jesus said to him, 'They have no wine.' And Jesus said to her, 'O woman, what have you to do with Me? My hour is not yet come.' His mother said to the servants, 'Do whatever he tells you'" (John 2:3–5). Jesus was not ready to perform the miracle, but out of obedience to His mother, He performs the miracle which is the first of a series of miracles in the Gospel of John. In Luke 8:19–21, she is mentioned together with Jesus' family in the Gospel text which is read at many of her feast days, "Then His mother and His brothers came to Him, but they could not reach him for the crowd. And He was told, 'Your mother and your brothers are standing outside, desiring to see You.' But He said to them, 'My mother and my brothers are those who hear the word of God and do it.'" She is also mentioned by the evangelist John as one of persons standing at the foot of the cross together with John the beloved disciple (John 19:25–27). In the Book of Acts 1:14, Mary is with the other disciples in the upper room after Jesus ascended into heaven. The Apostle Paul does not specifically mention her by name but refers to her as the mother of Jesus, "But when the time had fully come, God sent forth His Son, born of a woman, born under the law, to redeem those under the law, so that we may receive adoption as sons" (Galatians 4:4–7).

However, in the birth narratives she has a role, secondary only to that of Jesus. The Lord used her as His instrument of redemption and salvation. One of the most beautiful hymns in the Orthodox Church is the Magnifact, which is sung during the All-Night Vigil service. The Magnificat is taken directly from the first chapter of Luke's Gospel. When Mary visits Elizabeth, Elizabeth, who is already six months pregnant, realizes that Mary is carrying a very special child. She tells Mary, "Blessed are you among women and blessed is the fruit of your womb! And why is this granted to me, that the mother of my Lord should come to me? For behold, when the voice of your greeting came to my ears, the babe in my womb leaped for joy. And blessed is she who believed that there would be a fulfillment of what was spoken of her from the Lord" (Luke 1:42–45). Mary responded to Elizabeth with the following words:

> My soul magnifies the Lord, and my spirit rejoices in God my savior
> For He has regarded the low estate of His handmaiden,
> For behold all generations will call me blessed;
> For He who is mighty has done great things for me
> And holy is His name
> And His mercy is on those who fear Him
> From generation to generation
> He has shown strength with his arm
> He has scattered the proud in the imagination of their hearts
> He has put down the mighty from their thrones
> And exalted those of low degree
> He has filled the hungry with good things
> And the rich He has sent empty away
> He has helped His servant Israel
> In remembrance of His mercy
> As He spoke to our fathers
> To Abraham and to His posterity for ever.
> (Luke 1:46–55)

These words remind us of God's generous love toward His people. He exalts the humble and the lowly, and He brings down the mighty and the powerful, themes which are woven throughout the Old Testament. The Magnificat also echoes a very important Old Testament text which is found in 1 Samuel 2:1–10. Here, the once barren Hannah offers a prayer to God in thanksgiving for bearing a son with her husband Elknah. Her son is not just any child, but Samuel who will grow up to be one of the first prophets in the Old Testament. Samuel also is the one who anointed David to be the king. Note how both texts are very similar, the one from Luke drawing upon themes from the prayer from Hannah:

> My heart exults in the Lord:
> My strength is exalted in the Lord;
> My mouth derides my enemies,

Because I rejoice in Thy salvation.
There is none holy like the Lord,
There is none besides Thee;
There is no rock like our God.
Talk no more so very proudly,
Let not arrogance come from your mouth;
For the Lord is a God of knowledge
And by Him actions are weighed,
The bows of the might are broken,
But the feeble gird on strength.
Those who were full have hired
Themselves out for bread,
But those who were hungry have ceased to hunger.
The barren has borne seven,
But she who has many children is forlorn.
The Lord kills and brings to life;
He brings down to Sheol and raises up.
The Lord makes poor and makes rich;
He brings low, He also exalts.
He raises up the poor from the dust;
He lifts the needy from the ash heap
To make them sit with princes
And inherit a seat of honor.
For the pillars of the earth are the Lord's,
And on them He has set the world.
He will guard the feet of His faithful ones;
But the wicked shall be cut off in darkness;
For not by might shall a man prevail.
The adversaries of the Lord shall be broken to pieces
Against them He will thunder in heaven.
The Lord will judge the ends of the earth;
He will give strength to His king,
And exalt the power of His anointed.
(I Samuel 2:1–10).

Throughout the Scriptures, the biblical God uses that which is broken in the world as a tool for working out His salvation. He uses the barren Sarah in order to produce Isaac; He uses an orphan Israelite child named Moses to be the giver of the Law; He uses a young virgin girl named Mary to bear the Word of God, and He uses the Pharisee Saul who persecuted Christians who later becomes the first among the Apostles. With God, truly all things are possible.

We remember that while Mary has a central role in this season of Christmas, it is only because of her son that she receives her due honor and respect by Christians. Orthodox Christians rightfully refer to her as the "Theotokos," or (God-bearer), because she bore God's son Jesus Christ, who is both God and man. She is almost always depicted in icons with her son, because He is the savior and Lord. Mary is an example for all Christians, because she accepted the Word of God and kept it. We remember her during the days preceeding and following Christmas, and hopefully, as Luke tells us, all generations will call her blessed.

CHAPTER THREE

JOSEPH: THE MAN OF DREAMS
MATTHEW 1:18–25

Joseph said to the virgin:
What has happened to you, O Mary?
I am troubled; what can I say to you?
Doubt clouds my mind; depart from me!
What has happened to you, O Mary?
Instead of honor, you bring me shame.
Instead of joy, you fill me with grief.
Men who praised me will blame me.
I cannot bear condemnation from every side.
I received you, a pure virgin in the sight of
    the Lord.
What is that I now see?
— *Stikhera from First Hour of the
Royal Hours of Christmas*

On the first Sunday following Christmas, we commemorate three important persons: Joseph the betrothed, David the King and James the brother of the Lord. Outside the birth narratives, Joseph is mentioned only a few times, generally in reference to Jesus, Mary and the town of Nazareth:

And He closed the book, and gave it back to the attendant, and sat down; and the eyes of all in the synagogue were fixed on Him. And He began to say to them, "Today this Scripture has been fulfilled in your hearing." And all spoke well of Him, and wondered at the gracious words which proceeded out of His mouth; and they said, "Is not this Joseph's son?" (Luke 4:20–22. See also Mark 6:1–6; John 1:25, 6:42)

And when Jesus had finished these parables, He went away from there, and coming to His own country He taught them in their synagogue, so that they were astonished, and said, "Where did this man get this wisdom and these mighty works? Is not this the carpenter's son? Is not His mother called Mary? And are not His brothers and sisters with us? And they took offense at Him. But Jesus said to them, "A prophet is not without honor except in his own country and in his own house." And He did not do many mighty works there because of their unbelief (Matthew 13:53–58. See also John 19:19, Acts 2:22, 3:6, 4: 10, 6:14, 10:38, 22:8, 26:9).

We do not know much about Joseph other than what the Gospels tell us. He was from the line of David, he was a carpenter, and he lived in Nazareth with Mary. Furthermore, Matthew tells us that an angel announces the good news to Joseph that his wife Mary will bear a son:

Joseph, son of David, do not fear to take Mary your wife, for that which is conceived in her is of the Holy Spirit; she will bear a son, and you shall call His name Jesus, for He will save His people from their sins." And this took place to fulfill what the Lord had spoken by the prophet, "Behold, a virgin shall conceive and bear a son, and His name shall be called Emmanuel" (which means God with us). When Joseph woke from sleep, he did as the angel of the Lord commanded him; he took his wife, but knew her not until she had borne a son; and he called His name Jesus" (Matthew 1:18–25).

According to Matthew, Joseph has two more dreams: one in which an angel warns Joseph that Herod is seeking to kill the child Jesus, and another where an angel tells Joseph that it is now time to return home, "But when Herod died, behold, an angel of the Lord appeared in a dream to Joseph in Egypt, saying, "Rise, take the child and his mother, and go to the land of Israel, for those who sought the child's life are dead" (Matthew 2:19–20).

Dreams are very common throughout the Old Testament. For example, King Solomon is asked by the Lord in a dream what he wishes to have. When Solomon asks for wisdom, the Lord grants him this wish and in addition gives him wealth and power (1 Kings 3:5–15):

At Gibeon the Lord appeared to Solomon in a dream by night, and God said, "Ask what I shall give you." And Solomon said, "Thou hast shown great and steadfast love to Thy servant David my father, because he walked before Thee in faithfulness, in righteousness, and in uprightness of heart toward Thee; and Thou hast kept for him this great and steadfast love, and hast given him a son to sit on his throne this day. And now, O Lord my God, Thou hast made Thy servant king in place of David my father, although I am but a little child; I do not know how to go out or come in. And Thy servant is in the midst of Thy people whom Thou hast chosen, a great people, that cannot be numbered or counted for multitude. Give Thy servant therefore an understanding mind to govern Thy people, that I may discern between good and evil; for who is able to govern this Thy great people? (1 Kings 3:5–9).

The text goes on to say that upon his rising from sleep, Solomon offered burnt offerings and peace offerings in the temple for all the people. Likewise, Jacob had a dream at Bethel where he saw a ladder that reached far into the heavens and angels were ascending and descending on it. Then, the Lord told Jacob in the dream that He would bless Jacob and his descendents and that He would never leave Jacob:

Jacob left Beersheba, and went toward Haran. And he came to a certain place, and stayed there because the sun had set. Taking one of the stones of the place, he put it under his head and lay down in that place to sleep. And he dreamed that there was a ladder set upon on the earth and on the top of it reached to heaven, and behold, the angels of God were ascending and descending on it. And behold, the Lord stood above it and said, "I am the Lord, the God of Abraham your father, and the God of Isaac, the land on which you lie I will give to you and to your descendants, and your descendants shall be like the dust of the earth and you shall spread abroad to the west and to the east and to the north and to the south; and by you and your descendants shall all the families of the earth bless themselves. Behold, I am with you and will keep you wherever you go, and will bring you back to this land; for I will not leave you until I have done that of which I have spoken to you." Then Jacob awoke from his sleep and said, "Surely the Lord is in this place; and I did not know it." And he was afraid, and said, "How awesome is this place!" This is none other than the house of God, and this is the gate of heaven" (Genesis 28:10–17).

Not only are visions and dreams abundant in the Old Testament but also dream interpretation. While dreams are considered important, it is even more important to understand the meaning of these dreams. Daniel becomes the interpreter of dreams at the court of Nebuchadnezzar and foretells his demise (Daniel 2:36–45).

Matthew's description of Joseph, Mary's betrothed, is highly reminiscent of Joseph in the Old Testament, who was considered the man of dreams. He was the youngest son of Jacob and Rachel (Genesis 30:24;

35:24, and 1 Chronicles 2:2) and was envied and hated by his brothers in part because of his dreams:

> Now Joseph had a dream, and when he told it to his brothers they only hated him the more. He said to them, "Hear this dream which I have dreamed: behold, we were binding sheaves in the field, and lo, my sheaf arose and stood upright; and behold your sheaves gathered round it, and bowed down to my sheaf." His brother said to him, "Are you indeed to reign over us? Or are you indeed to have dominion over us? So they hated him yet more for his dreams and for his words. Then he dreamed another dream; and behold, the sun, the moon, and the eleven stars were bowing down to me." But when he told it to his father and to his brothers his father rebuked him, and said to him, "What is this dream that you have dreamed? Shall I and your mother and your brothers indeed come bow ourselves to the ground before you?" and his brothers were jealous of him, but his father kept the saying in mind (Genesis 37:5–12).

Joseph's role in Matthew's birth story is prominent. He is a "just man" and obedient to the word of God. Joseph doubts the truthfulness of his wife's pregnancy, just as Moses doubts his new role as the law-giver and as Sarah doubts the conception of her son Isaac. Yet, Joseph, like Moses and Sarah, remains faithful to the Lord, trusts in God's plan, listens to the word of God and follows it by taking his family and raising them in the town of Nazareth.

Now, I venture to say that most of us do not have dreams like Joseph. If we did, I am sure not many of our friends would believe us — they would probably send us to a doctor to get help! Conventional wisdom tells us that otherworldly visions and dreams are "ultra-spiritual" and mysterious and are wonderful ways to experience our faith. Yet, I am not so sure that we should be seeking visions of Jesus or Mary, or anyone else for that matter. After all, the Scriptures remind us that even the devil can come to us as an angel of light (2 Cor. 11:14). We cannot be certain that our dreams and visions are from God; therefore, we should not dwell on them. Many of the saints say that if you have a spiritual vision or dream do not tell anyone, just say a prayer, and forget about it. In other words, our faith is not in dreams and visions but in Jesus Christ crucified who comes to us through His spoken Word in the Scriptures and in the liturgy of the Church.

It is here, in the saving message of the Word of God, where we encounter the everlasting and life-giving good news of the Kingdom if we choose to listen. We must have open hearts so the seed of the Gospel can be planted in it. As Matthew says, the good soil receives the seed, and it takes root. Hopefully, the Word will take root in our hearts and grow abundantly.

CHAPTER FOUR

WE ARE FAMILY
MATTHEW 1:1–17

Mary was of David's seed,
So she went with Joseph to register in Bethlehem
She bore in her womb the fruit not sown by man
The time for the birth was at hand
Since there was no room at the inn
The cave became a beautiful palace for the queen
Christ was born, raising up the image that fell of old.
— *Troparion of the Royal Hours for Christmas*

When I was in junior high school, I was interested in my family heritage. My Uncle Edward had researched our family tree and sent me a copy. He traced our family history back to a small village in Denmark. This was a surprise since I had always thought that we were Norwegian! Apparently, my father was wrong all of those years, but that was okay — Danes are fellow Vikings and neighbors to the Norwegians. I imagined that my ancestors were Viking explorers who traveled across the globe looking for adventure and treasure. I was also interested in how our family came to the United States. Uncle Edward learned that his mother, Elsie Jorgensen, had sailed across the Atlantic with her sister to seek a new life and a husband in the New World. My grandmother Elsie died before I was born, so I never had the opportunity to meet her, but I always saw her picture in our house. I could not believe that she traveled across the Atlantic; she must have been a strong person. I only knew grandmother Elsie through her pictures and through stories about her that I learned from my Uncle Edward. At some time in our life, usually in our youth, we begin to wonder where we came from, how we got here, and who are our ancestors. These are the same basic questions about family origins which have been asked for millennia. People across the globe have looked to their past in order to explain how they arrived in their present situation.

On the Sunday before Christmas, we hear a reading from the Gospel of Matthew which includes a long list of names in Jesus' family tree, or a "genealogy." A genealogy is a fancy name for the study of families. The Old Testament contains many genealogies, especially in 1–2 Kings and in 1 Chronicles 1–9. Many of the names such as Shimni, Jedaiah and Jehu may seem strange to us since they are not very common in our modern era. The author of 1 Chronicles gives us a genealogy of the first patriarch Abraham: "The sons of Abraham: Isaac and Ishmael. These are their genealogies: the first born of Ishmael, Nebaioth; and Kedar, Abdeel, Misbam, Mishma, Dumah, Massa, Hadad, Tema, Jetur, Naphish, and Kedemah. These are the sons of Ishmael, the sons of Keturah, Abraham's concubine: she bore Zimran, Jokshan, Medan, Midian, Ishbak, and Shuah" (1 Chronicles 1:28–33). These lists identify someone within the larger family tree together with their extended family and their offspring.

In the New Testament, we have two different genealogies, one in Matthew 1:1–17 and the other in Luke 3:23–38. Luke begins with Joseph and traces the lineage of Jesus back to the first man Adam, while Matthew begins with Jesus and traces his family through the lineage of both the great King David and through Abraham, the first patriarch. Luke's genealogy includes only men, while Matthew includes both men and women. Matthew and Luke wrote their genealogies for different purposes in mind, and therefore, we should not be surprised that there are differences between the two genealogies.[2] Jesus did not appear from just anywhere, but was from a specific family and was born in a particular time and place with a particular family. The prophet Isaiah alludes to the root of Jesse in his prophecies to Israel, which are also read during the services for Great Compline on Christmas Eve:

> The people who walked in darkness have seen a great light; those who
> dwelt in a land of deep darkness, on them has light shined. Thou has

---

[2] The reader is encouraged to read both genealogies and look up the various names in both lists. Many of the persons mentioned were important in the rise of God's people Israel in the Old Testament.

multiplied the nation, thou has increased its joy; they rejoice before Thee as with joy at the harvest, as men rejoice when they divide the spoil. From the yoke of his burden, and the staff for his shoulder, the rod of his oppressor, Thou has broken as on the day of Midian. For every boot of the trampling warriors in battle tumult and every garment rolled in blood will be burned as fuel for the fire. For to us a child is born, to us a son is given; and the government will be upon His shoulder, and His name will be called "Wonderful Counselor, Mighty God, Everlasting Father, Prince of Peace." Of the increase of His government and of peace there will be no end, upon the throne of David, and over his kingdom, to establish it, and to uphold it with justice and with righteousness from this time forth and forevermore. The zeal of the Lord of hosts will do this (Isaiah 9:2–7).

There shall come forth a shoot from the stump of Jesse, and a branch shall grow out of his roots. And the Spirit of the Lord shall rest upon him, the Spirit of wisdom and understanding, the spirit of counsel and might, the spirit of knowledge and the fear of the Lord. And his delight shall be in the fear of the Lord. He shall not judge by what his eyes see, or decide by what his ears hear; but with righteousness he shall judge the poor, and decide with equity for the meek of the earth; and he shall smite the earth with the rod of his mouth, and with the breath of his lips he shall slay the wicked. Righteousness shall be the girdle of his waist, and faithfulness the girdle of his loins. The wolf shall dwell with the lamb, and the leopard shall lie down with the kid, and the calf and the lion together, and a little child shall lead them, the cow and the bear shall feed; their young shall lie down together; and the lion shall eat straw like the ox. The suckling child shall play over the hole of the asp, and the weaned child shall put his hand on the adder's den. They shall not hurt or destroy in my holy mountain; for the earth shall be full of the knowledge of the Lord as the waters cover the sea. In that day the root of Jesse shall stand as an ensign to the peoples; him shall the nations seek, and his dwelling shall be glorious (Isaiah 11:1–10).

Isaiah also says that all nations will bow down and worship God, because He is faithful to His word and will not allow Israel's enemies to subdue them: "And the Lord will utterly destroy the tongue of the sea of Egypt; and will wave His hand over the River with His scorching wind, and smite it into seven channels that men may cross dryshod" (Isaiah 11:15). Isaiah spoke of a messiah who will bring both peace and justice, as the ox and lamb lie together so too will the messiah bring enemies together. Isaiah's prophecy was fulfilled in the birth of Jesus who brings the eternal peace of God to both Jew and Gentile, slave and free, man and woman.

Matthew also mentions King David in the genealogy. King David was also one of the greatest and most beloved kings of the Old Testament. In his youth, David was a shepherd boy and musician who slew the giant Goliath. He was the youngest of Jesse's eight sons and was anointed a king by the prophet Samuel:

> When they came, he looked on Eliab and thought, "Surely the Lord's anointed is before him." But the Lord said to Samuel, "Do not look on his appearance or on the height of his stature, because I have rejected him; for the Lord sees not as a man sees; man looks on the outward appearance, but the Lord looks on the heart." Then Jesse called Aminadab, and made him pass before Samuel. And he said, "Neither has the Lord chosen this one." Then Jesse made Shammah pass by. And he said, "Neither has the Lord chosen this one." And Jesse made seven of his sons pass before Samuel. And Samuel said to Jesse, "The Lord has not chosen these." And Samuel said to Jesse, "Are all your sons here?" And he said, "There remains yet the youngest, but behold, he is keeping the sheep." And Samuel said to Jesse, "Send and fetch him; for we will not sit down till he comes." And he sent, and brought him in. Now he was ruddy, and had beautiful eyes, and was handsome. And the Lord said, "Arise, anoint him, for this is he." Then Samuel took the horn of oil, and anointed him in the midst of his brothers, and the Spirit of the Lord came mightily upon David from that day forward. And Samuel rose up and went to Ramah (1 Samuel 16:10–13. See also 2 Samuel 5:1–5).

As King, he led the Israelites in battle and provided justice and equity among the peoples. The Book of Psalms is attributed to him (1 Samuel 16:14; 17:1). In the New Testament, Jesus is often mentioned in connection with King David, "And as Jesus passed on from there, two blind men followed Him crying aloud, "Have mercy on us, Son of David" (Matthew 9:27. See also Luke 18:38, John 7:42, and 2 Timothy 2: 8). However, King David also had a dark side; he fell into sin after he had Uriah sent to his death on the battlefield so that he could sleep with Uriah's wife Bathsheeba. Yet, even though David did a terrible thing, he repented and was obedient to God.

Matthew also links Jesus with the first patriarch Abraham, who is mentioned three times in the birth narratives (Matthew 1:1, 2, 17).

Abraham is an important person in the Old Testament, because the covenant (promise) was first given to him that he would be the father of all nations: "Now the Lord said to Abram, 'Go forth from your country and your kindred and your father's house to the land that I will show you. And I will make you a great nation, and I will bless you, and make your name great, so that you will be a blessing. I will bless those who bless you, and him who curses you I will curse; and by your all the families of the earth shall bless themselves'" (Genesis 12:1–3. See also Isaiah 19:24, Acts 3:25–26, Romans 4:13). Abraham is important, because it is through his offspring that God will provide His blessing. Thus, God fulfills His promise-covenant through Abraham.

While Matthew's genealogy clearly connects Jesus with both the kingly Davidic line and with the Abrahamic covenant, Matthew also includes four noteworthy women in Jesus' family: Rahab, Ruth, Tamar and Mary. Rahab was a harlot from Jericho who helped two spies escape the city of Jericho (Joshua 2:1–24); Ruth was a Moabite who lived among the Israelites, the Moabites were considered outsiders (Ruth 1:1–5); Tamar was a Canaanite women who disguised herself as a prostitute in order to seduce Judah (Gen 38:1ff); and Mary was an unwed bride who bore Jesus. All of these women were strong yet also provided opportunities for God to work His salvation through their actions. These women were also obedient and faithful to the Lord. Ruth remained close to her mother-in-law Naomi when Naomi's son died; Tamar married Judah who later became one of the great leaders of the southern Kingdom; and Mary accepted then angel's message that she would bear the son of God.

Matthew's genealogy shows us that Jesus' family was certainly a motley crew. Jesus' family included all types of people: political leaders, kings, queens, gentiles, sinners, not to mention murders, harlots, liars and other unsavory types of people. Perhaps, Matthew is trying to tell us that Jesus comes from a very human family, not very different from families like ours. Yet, it is through this human family that God chooses to bring His salvation. Specifically, the biblical God wants His salvation through the sinners and outsiders on the margins of society, especially the poor, widow, orphan and outsider. Jesus comes to those who are not accepted in society and shows His love in concrete ways. He eats with sinners, speaks with outsiders and is a friend of harlots. Jesus goes out of His way to welcome those in society whom no one else will welcome. He provides us with the best example of how to show hospitality to strangers. One of Jesus' names attributed to Him in the birth narratives is Emmanuel, which means, "God with us." During the Christmas season, we are reminded that God is truly with us and finds His home in our strange human family.

CHAPTER FIVE

GLORY TO GOD IN THE HIGHEST

LUKE 2:9–14

> Before Thy birth, O Lord,
> The hosts of angels already perceived the mystery.
> They were struck with wonder and trembled,
> For Thou who didst adorn the heavens with stars
> Art now well pleased to be born as a babe.
> Thou holdest the ends of the earth in Thy hands,
> But now Thou art laid in a manger of dumb beasts.
> Yet all these things fulfilled Thy saving plan,
> By which Thy compassion was revealed to us.
> O Christ of great mercy, glory to Thee!
> — *Stikhera for Third Hour of the Royal Hours of Christmas*

I have never encountered an angel of the Lord. The only angels that I have seen are on television shows like "Highway to Heaven" and "Touched by an Angel," where Michael Landon and Della Reese interceded on behalf of humans in strange or dangerous predicaments. Our understanding of angels has been formed by television programs and by our popular culture, which presents angels as chubby little cherubs floating around on flags, greeting cards, tapestries and banners. Here, they seem cute, harmless and other wordly, what we call "spiritual." However, when reading the Scriptures, especially the birth narratives, we have an altogether different depiction of angels. This image is sometimes a fearful one since angels are God's servants and come on His behalf. Thus, in the Scripture, when someone encounters an angel, they usually react in fear.

Nine months before the birth of Jesus, the angel Gabriel came to Mary and told her that she was going to bear the son of God. Luke records this scene in the following manner, "And he came to her and said, 'Hail, O favored one, the Lord is with you!' But she was greatly troubled at the saying, and considered in her mind what sort of greeting this might be. And the angel said to her, 'Do not be afraid, Mary, for you have found favor with God. And behold, you will conceive in your womb and bear a son, and you shall call His name Jesus'" (Luke 1:26–31). Luke continues by telling us that Mary accepted this invitation and pondered these words in her heart. The annunciation story is a familiar one and has been the subject for numerous works of art and poetry.

Throughout the Scriptures, angels invoke fear in people. In his vision of the heavenly throne room, Isaiah vividly describes Seraphim and Cherubim flying around the heavenly throne singing, "Holy, holy, holy, is the Lord of hosts; the whole earth is full of His glory" (Isaiah 6:3). In his vision, the earth is shaking and the temple is filled with smoke. Isaiah is not excited or happy to behold the glory of the Lord. Instead, he responds with fear, "Woe is me! For I am lost; for I am a man of unclean lips, and I dwell in the midst of a people of unclean lips, for my eyes have seen the King, the Lord of hosts" (Isaiah 6:5).

On the first Easter morning, when the myrhhbearing women arrive at the tomb to anoint Jesus' body, they meet an angel and also react out of fear:

> And behold there was a great earthquake; for an angel of the Lord descended from heaven and came and rolled away the stone, and sat upon it. His appearance was like lightning, and his raiment white as snow. And for fear of him the guards trembled and became like dead men. But the angel said to the women, "Do not be afraid; for I know that you seek Jesus who was crucified. He is not here, for He has risen as He said. Come, see the place where he lay. Then go quickly and tell his disciples that He has risen from the dead, and behold He is going before you to Galilee, there you will see Him. Lo, I have told you" (Matthew 28:1–7).

When the women encountered the angel, they were afraid; after all, they came to the tomb expecting to see their Lord and Master, but instead they found this heavenly messenger who told them to let the disciples know that Jesus is risen.

The word "angel" means messenger, and people react from fear because they are encountering not just a heavenly being, but a word from God. Encountering God's word is like encountering God Himself, you are hearing Him speak, which is a fearful thing as Isaiah noted in his vision of the throne room. When Jonah was called to prophesy to the people of Nineveh, he fled to Tarshish instead in order to get away from God. The rest of the Jonah story reveals that eventually, Jonah found himself preaching to the people of Nineveh and obeying the Lord. Likewise, it took God two times to get Jeremiah to prophesy to the people of Israel, because Jeremiah was too stubborn to preach since he considered himself too young for the job. God thought otherwise.

At Jesus' birth, the angels announce to the shepherds the good news that the Christ child is born. The Gospel is "good news" and is given to the shepherds so that they too may go and see the Savior and Lord. When they hear the good news from the angels about the Christ child, they too react out of fear:

> And in that region there were shepherds out in the field, keeping watch over their flock by night. And an angel of the Lord appeared to them, and the glory of the Lord shone around them, and they were filled with fear. And an angel of the Lord said to them, "Be not afraid; for behold, I bring you good news of great joy which will come to all the people; for to you is born this day in the city of David a Savior, who is Christ the Lord. And this will be a sign for you: you will find a babe wrapped in swaddling cloths and lying in a manger" (Luke 2:8–13).

The angelic message may at first seem fearful, but it is really a message of hope. The angels announce that the Christ child will bring peace to the world which is long overdue. However, this peace is not the peace of the Roman Empire, the peace of kings, rulers, politicians and soldiers — but the heavenly peace, the peace of God. This is the peace of Christ, the peace from God Himself of which the prophet Isaiah speaks: "The wolf shall dwell with the lamb, and the leopard will lie down with the kid, and the calf and the fatling together, and a little child shall lead them" (Isaiah 11:6). We are given this message of peace during Christmas as a reminder that we are called to maintain and cultivate this peace throughout our lives. It is not always an easy task, since we encounter many roadblocks in life. Yet, we know that the only peace that matters is the peace of God which will always prevail. May we always seek the peace of Christ, now at the season of Christmas, and throughout the year, for this is the only peace that matters in this world.

CHAPTER SIX

SHEPHERDS KEEPING WATCH

LUKE 2:8–20

> When the Lord Jesus was born of the holy virgin,
> The whole universe was filled with light.
> The shepherds watched in the fields.
> The wise men worshipped and the angels sang.
> But Herod was troubled,
> For God appeared in the flesh.
> He is the Savior of our souls!
> — *Stikhera on Lord I Call Vesperal Divine*
> *Liturgy of St. Basil the Great*

Two summers ago, my wife and I traveled through the back roads of Scotland and England on our annual summer vacation. We drove through hundreds of miles of lush green fields filled with poppies and lavender and also past many farms full of cows, horses and, of course, lots of sheep. One of Scotland's claim to fame is that they boast of having more sheep than people!

Shepherds have a difficult job. Sheep need constant care and attention, and lots of food and water. They also have to be shorn regularly so that their coats do not get too thick. The shearing process is tedious, taking lots of manual labor and patience. The shorn wool then has to be sent to local mills for processing where it is turned into scarves, hats, sweaters, blankets and other textile products. Shepherding is not a high paying job, many shepherds supplement their jobs with farming or some other line of work. While we may live in a modern society, the art of shepherding has not changed much throughout time. During Jesus' time, shepherding was a job for the poor. It still takes vigilance, patience and lots of work. Interestingly, according to Luke, the angels first announce the glad tidings of the birth of the Savior to shepherds keeping watch in the fields. Thus, the Gospel first comes to the poor and lowly shepherds of Israel.

However, shepherds are not always portrayed in the best of light in the Scriptures. The prophet Ezekiel speaks against the shepherds of Israel, who are considered the leaders of the people, for not taking care of their flocks:

> The word of the Lord came to me, "Son of man, prophesy against the shepherds of Israel, prophesy, and say to them, even to the shepherds, Thus says the Lord, 'You eat the fat, you clothe yourselves with the wool, you slaughter the fatlings, but you do not feed the sheep. The weak you have not healed, the crippled you have not bound up, the strayed you have not brought back, the lost you have not sought, and with force and harshness you have ruled them.' So they were scattered, because there was no shepherd, and they became food for all the wild beasts. My sheep were scattered, they wandered over all the mountains and on every high hill; my sheep were scattered over all the face of the earth, with none to search or seek for them (Ezekiel 34:1–4).

Ezekiel continues as he blames the shepherds for the woes of the poor and the destitute and blames the leaders for neglecting to take care of them. In other words, the shepherds were too busy taking care of themselves rather than taking care those under their charge.

This theme of shepherding is also developed within the New Testament. In the Gospel of John, Jesus is called the "good shepherd," the one who leads His flock to pasture and who protects the flock even if it means sacrificing His own life. As the good shepherd, Jesus cares for His flock as the shepherds in Ezekiel could not: "I am the good shepherd. The good shepherd lays down His life for the sheep. He who is a hireling and not a shepherd, whose own the sheep are not, sees the wolf coming and leaves the sheep and flees, and the wolf snatches them and scatters them. He flees because he is a hireling and cares nothing for the sheep" (John 10:11–13). While there are many shepherds, there is only one good shepherd, Jesus Christ. One of the shortest, but also most comforting of the Psalms, is Psalm 23 where God Himself is referred to as a shepherd:

The Lord is my shepherd I shall not want;
He makes me lie down in green pastures.
He leads me beneath still waters;
He restores my soul.
He leads me in paths of righteousness
For His name's sake
Even though I walk through the valley of the shadow of death,
I fear no evil;
For Thou art with me;
Thy rod and Thy staff
They comfort me
Thou preparest a table before me
In the presence of my enemies
Thou anointest my head with oil
My cup overflows
Surely goodness and mercy shall follow me
All the days of my life
And I shall dwell in the house of the Lord for ever.
(Psalm 23)

This Psalm is comforting to many people who are in distress, especially during times of sorrow and grief. The Psalmist speaks of the shepherd as leading, restoring and comforting, words which bring solace to people who are hurt.

However, the Scriptures also speak of the shepherding in terms of judgment. In Matthew 25, the king will separate the sheep from the goats, as a shepherd routinely does in order to keep his flock safe: "When the Son of Man comes in His glory, and all the angels with Him, then He will sit on His glorious throne. Before Him will be gathered all the nations, and He will separate them one from another as a shepherd separates the sheep from the goats, and He will place the sheep at His right hand, but the goats on His left" (Matthew 25:31–33). The reality is that the good shepherd, the Son of God, will come with ultimate power and authority to execute His divine judgment in the world.

We are not told whether the shepherds in the birth narratives are good or bad, just that they were in their fields keeping watch over their flocks. Luke tells us that they are the first ones to hear the good news. This child is the messiah of God who comes to bring peace and justice in the world. He will grow up to be the "good shepherd" who leads His followers to the Kingdom and who rules with justice and equity, so that the "increase of His government and of peace there will be no end, upon the throne of David, and over His kingdom to establish it, and to uphold it with justice and with righteousness from this time forth and for evermore" (Isaiah 9:7). The ultimate message is that this Christ child, who is born in Bethlehem, will also bring His justice and peace to the entire world.

CHAPTER SEVEN

BETHLEHEM

LUKE 2:1–7

Make ready, O Bethlehem.
Let the manger be prepared.
Let the cave show its welcome.
The truth comes and the shadow flees.
God is born of a virgin and revealed to men.
He is clothed in our flesh, and makes it divine
Therefore Adam is renewed, and cries out with Eve
Thy favor has appeared on earth, O Lord.
For the salvation of the human race.
— *Stikhera from First Hour of the*
Royal Hours of Christmas

Every Christmas Eve, there is a televised evening Church service broadcast from the Church of the Nativity in Bethlehem. This event draws hundreds of pilgrims and faithful Christians who want to be a part of a very special service in the birthplace of our Lord. While inside the Church there is safety and solemnity in the hymns and prayers, outside the Church there is chaos. Bethlehem is located in the middle of the occupied territory where millions of Palestinian Arabs, many of them Orthodox Christians, cannot move around freely. Neither can they obtain gainful employment. Their lives are restricted to the maximum. At the writing of this book, the Israeli government is erecting a high fence that will greatly restrict the movement of the Palestinian Arabs. If this fence is completed, it will create a social and economic barrier and an ethnic and religious ghetto in that part of the world. Unfortunately, not much has changed in two thousand years — the poor are still oppressed and impoverished while those in the government use their military and political power to remain in control, restricting the economic, political and religious future of those under their charge.

During Jesus' lifetime, the Roman government controlled all of the Mediterranean world. The Romans had the most powerful empire at that time, and their soldiers were equipped with the best weapons. This power was not achieved overnight. It took years of battle and warfare to gain political and military supremacy. But after many wars and much bloodshed, the new emperor, Augustus Caesar, declared that the doors of the Temple of Janus would be closed, and there would be a new era of peace, known as the *Pax Romana*.[3] This is the same Augustus Caesar mentioned in the beginning of Luke, chapter two, "In those days a decree went out from Caesar Augustus that all the world should be enrolled" (Luke 2:1). Archeological evidence shows that on his statues were found the words "god" and "savior" pointing toward his power and authority throughout the empire. Compared with the wealth and power of the Roman aristocracy, the majority of the population were peasants and lived in poverty. There was much homelessness and hunger, and few jobs paid a living wage. In previous generations, the prophets spoke out against the oppression of the poor:

> Hear this, you who trample upon the needy, and bring the poor of the land to an end, saying, "When will the new moon be over, that we may sell grain? And the Sabbath, that we may offer wheat for sale, that we may make the ephah small and the shekel great, and deal deceitfully with false balances, that we may buy the poor for silver and the needy for a pair of sandals, and sell the refuse of the wheat?" (Amos 8:4–6)

> They hate him who reproves in the gate and they abhor him who speaks the truth. Therefore because you trample upon the poor and take from him exactions of wheat, you have built houses hewn of stone but you shall not dwell in them, you have planted pleasant vineyards, but you shall not drink their wine. For I know how many are your transgressions, and how great are your sins-you who afflict the righteous, who take a bribe, and turn aside the needy in the gate.

---

[3] Janus was the Roman god of war. During times of war, the doors of the temple were open, allowing people to come and offer sacrifices to Janus to lead their armies in battle. During times of peace, the doors of the temple were closed. The *Pax Romana* means the Roman Peace.

> Therefore, he who is prudent will keep silent in such a time; for it is an evil time. Seek good and not evil, that you may live; and so the Lord, the God of hosts, will be with you, as you have said. Hate evil, and love good, and establish justice in the gate; it may be that the Lord, the God of hosts, will be gracious to the remnant of Joseph (Amos 5:10–15).

Amos was emphatic about helping the poor and needy. He railed against those who oppressed the poor and the disadvantaged. However, there is hope because the biblical God is always concerned about the poor and the lowly. He promises to send His anointed one (the Messiah) to protect the poor and the orphans and to bring down the proud in heart. The prophet Micah tells us that this anointed one will come from Bethlehem:

> Thus, says the Lord: But you, Bethlehem, house of Ephratha, are little among the thousands of Judah, yet from you shall come forth to me Him who is to be ruler in Israel, and His going forth is from the beginning, from the days of eternity. So the Lord will abandon His people to their enemies until the time when she who is in travail has given birth, then the remnant of His brethren will be converted to the children of Israel. And He shall stand, and feed His flock in the strength of the Lord and they shall abide in the glory of the name of the Lord their God, and they shall magnify Him even to the ends of the earth (Micah 5:2–4).

Bethlehem was the birthplace of David, one of the great Old Testament kings, and the place where the prophet Samuel anointed David to be the king (1 Samuel 16:4). Likewise, Bethlehem is where Ruth came to live with Naomi, her mother-in-law. Ruth was a Moabite who came to live with the Israelites, which was against the social custom of the time. Yet, Naomi welcomed Ruth into her house (Ruth 1:1–2:23). Furthermore, Ephratha was the burial place of Rachel, the wife of Jacob: "So Rachel died, and she was buried on the way to Ephrath (that is Bethlehem), and Jacob set up a pillar upon her grave, it is the pillar of Rachel's tomb, which is there to this day. Israel journeyed on, and pitched his tent beyond the tower of Eder" (Genesis 15:19). Thus, Bethlehem produced one of the greatest kings in the Old Testament and was where outsiders could live with the Israelites. It is here in this small part of the world, in a far away place called Bethlehem, where God chose to take flesh and make His home among us.

CHAPTER EIGHT

MAGI FROM THE EAST

MATTHEW 2:1–12

The wise men, kings from Persia,
Perceived without any doubt
That Thou was born on earth, O Heavenly King.
Drawn by the light of a star, they hurried to Bethlehem.
They offered Thee acceptable gifts:
Gold, myrhh, and frankincense.
They fell down before Thee and worshipped Thee,
Seeing Thee, the timeless One,
Lying in the cave as an infant
— *Stikhera on Litya Great Compline for the Feast of Christmas*

Matthew tells us that wise men from the East came bearing gifts of gold, frankincense and myrhh for the Christ child. In the medieval period, the tradition developed that there were three wise men whose names were Melchior, Casper and Balthasar. They later became subjects for the Christmas song "We Three Kings," which is often sung at Christmas tableaus and plays. Over a period of time, stories developed about the magi and their journeys. Some stories say that originally, there were four wise men who came to visit Jesus, however, along the way, one got lost. After many years traveling, searching for the baby Jesus, the wise man found his way to Jerusalem. In Jerusalem he heard about a man who was being crucified that day, it was Jesus.[4]

Matthew does not specify the names of the wise men, nor does he mention that there were three, but only that wise men came from the East:

---

[4] See the collected works in Pegram Johnson and Enda Troiano, *The Roads From Bethlehem: Christmas Literature from Writers Ancient and Modern* (Louisville, KY: Westminister/John Knox Press, 1993).

Now when Jesus was born in Bethlehem of Judea in the days of Herod the king, behold, wise men from the East came to Jerusalem, saying, "Where is He who has been born king of the Jews? For we have seen His star in the East, and have come to worship Him..." When they saw the star, they rejoiced exceedingly with great joy; and going into the house they fell down and worshipped Him. Then, opening their treasures, they offered Him gifts, gold and frankincense and myrrh. And being warned in a dream not to return to Herod, they departed to their own country by another way (Matthew 2:1–3, 10–12).

I see Him, but not now; I behold Him, but not nigh: a star shall come forth out of Jacob, and a scepter shall rise out of Israel; it shall crush the forehead of Moab, and break down all the sons of Sheth. Edome shall be dispossessed, Seir also, His enemies, shall be dispossessed, while Israel does valiantly. By Jacob shall dominion be exercised, and the survivors of cities be destroyed (Genesis 24:17–19. See also Numbers 24:2–3, 5–9, 17–18).

The only details we have about the wise men are that they came seeking to worship the baby Jesus and that when they saw the star in the East, they rejoiced with exceedingly great joy (Matthew 2:10). The fact that they are from the "east" and that they are "wise men" suggests that they are sages or astrologers from a Gentile background. In the ancient world, the sage or wise man, sometimes called a seer, was an advisor to the king or emperor. These people were the educated elite and were familiar with astrology as well as the natural sciences, literature and culture. Wise men or magi were usually connected with the royal palace.

Matthew also tells us that these wise men brought gifts of gold, frankincense and myrrh. These items may seem like strange gifts for a newborn child, but they have a special function within the birth story and the Gospel narrative as a whole. Myrrh is very similar to a heavy perfume and was very expensive, only the wealthy could afford it. Myrrh was frequently used for preparing bodies for burial. We know from the four Gospels that the women came to the tomb in order to anoint Jesus' body, "When the Sabbath was past, Mary Magdalene, and Mary the mother of James and Salome, bought spices, so that they might go an anoint Him" (Mark 16:1. See also Luke 24:1 and John 19:39). In the Orthodox tradition, these women are known as the myrrhbearing women.[5]

---

[5] The myrrhbearing women are commemorated on the second Sunday after Pascaha (Easter).

Likewise, both gold and frankincense were also expensive materials and were frequently used in the ancient world. Gold, of course, was used by the wealthy in society, and frankincense is a type of incense which was burned as a fragrant offering as we hear at every Vespers service: "I call upon Thee, O Lord; make haste to me! Give ear to my voice, when I call to Thee! Let my prayer be counted as incense before Thee, and the lifting of my hands as an evening sacrifice!" (Psalm 141:2). The appearance of the magi at the birth story echoes an important passage in Isaiah, where he describes that all nations will come together in order to bow down and pay homage to the Lord Almighty. They will bring gold and incense to the Lord:

> Arise, shine, for your light has come, and the glory of the Lord has risen upon you. For behold darkness shall cover the earth, and thick darkness the peoples; but the Lord will arise upon you and His glory will be seen upon you. And nations shall come to your light, and kings to the brightness of your rising. Lift up your eyes round about, and see, they all gather together, they come to you; your sons shall come from far, and your daughters shall be carried in the arms. Then you shall see and be radiant, your heart shall thrill and rejoice; because the abundance of the sea shall be turned to you, the wealth of nations shall come to you. A multitude of camels shall cover you, the young camels of Midian and Epaph; all those from Sheba shall come. They shall bring gold and frankincense, and shall proclaim the praise of the Lord. All the flocks of Kedar shall be gathered to you, the rams of Nebaioth shall minister to you; they come on my altar, and I will glorify my glorious house (Isaiah 60:1–7).

The appearance of the wise men remind us that this birth is unlike other births, because the child is going to be the savior of the world: "He will be great, and He will be called the Son of the Most High: and the Lord God will give to Him the throne of His father David, and He will reign over the house of Jacob for ever; and of His kingdom there will be no end" (Luke 1:32–33). Thus, the gift of salvation is announced to both the Jews, who are represented in the birth story by the shepherds in the fields, and to the Gentiles, who are represented by the magi. Both the shepherds and magi accept the invitation to see the Christ child, and both pay homage to Him. Matthew's birth story reminds us that the good news of salvation is offered to all peoples, or as Isaiah says, all nations. Hopefully, all nations will accept this wonderful invitation and bow down to God's beloved Son Jesus.

CHAPTER NINE

KING HEROD AND THE HOLY INNOCENTS
MATTHEW 2:16–18

Herod was filled with alarm
When he saw the righteous wisemen.
Overcome by fury,
He determined when the child was born
Mothers were robbed of their infants:
Their tender lives were reaped as a bitter harvest.
Milk stopped flowing and breasts dried up
Great was the suffering!
Therefore assemble in holy fear, O faithful,
To worship the birth of Christ!
— *Stikhera for Ninth Hour of the Royal Hours of Christmas*

The story of King Herod and the death of the holy innocents stands out grimly in the birth narratives. While Herod is never seen in crèche scenes and he seldom is represented in parish tableaus, he is mentioned in the birth narrative. While King Herod is not formally commemorated on the Church calendar, we do remember the martyrdom of the holy innocents in Bethlehem on December 29.

King Herod was King Herod the Great, the father of the Herodian dynasty and the father of Herod Antipas, who killed John the Baptist and assisted Pontius Pilate in condemning Jesus to death (Luke 9:7, 23:6–7). The Scriptures offer little information about King Herod except that he was the King of the Jews. The Jewish historian Josephus tells us that Herod was an ambitious politician and a strong leader.[6] He was alive when Julius Caesar was killed, and befriended Mark Antony.

---

[6] Josephus was a famous Jewish historian that lived from 37–101 C.E. and wrote numerous books about Judaism and early Christianity.

Herod was later summoned to Rome to receive the title "King of the Jews," and he returned to Jerusalem as their king. By the time of the birth of Jesus, the Roman Empire controlled most of the known world around the Mediterranean and was organized into smaller kingdoms. Herod, the king of Judea, was unpopular with many Jews because he was a foreigner and only part Jewish. Although Matthew does not tell us directly, it is likely that any news about a newborn king would not be welcomed by Herod or his followers. The mere mention of a newborn "king" would cause anxiety in most people, and especially to someone such as the unpopular Herod.

Herod told the wise men that he too wanted to visit the Christ child, "Then Herod summoned the wise men secretly and ascertained from them what time the star appeared and he sent them to Bethlehem, saying, 'Go and search diligently for the child, and when you have found Him bring me word, that I too may come and worship him'" (Matthew 2:7–8). Joseph took Mary and the infant Jesus and fled to Egypt, where they remained until the angel told them to return to Nazareth.

Herod, in a rage, had all the male children who were two years old or younger killed so that he could kill the baby Jesus. According to Matthew, this fulfills a prophecy in Jeremiah, "A voice was heard in Ramah, wailing and loud lamentation, Rachel weeping for her children; she refused to be consoled, because they were no more. Thus says the Lord: 'Keep your voice from weeping, and your eyes from tears; for your work shall be rewarded says the Lord, and they shall come back from the land of the enemy. There is hope for your future, says the Lord, and your children shall come back to their own country'" (Jeremiah 31:15). Jeremiah speaks of the exile of the northern tribes and uses the example of Rachel weeping for her children who were taken away.

The story of Herod and the holy innocents is strikingly similar to the beginning of the Exodus story. In Exodus, Pharoah wanted all the male babies killed because the Israelites were overpopulating Egypt. Yet, we know that Moses was miraculously saved, ironically, by Pharoah's daughter:

> Then Pharoah commanded all his people, "Every son that is born to the Hebrews you shall cast into the Nile, but you shall let

every daughter live." Now a man from the house of Levi went and took to wife a daughter of Levi. The woman conceived and bore a son, and when she saw that he was a godly child, she hid him three months. And when she could hide him no longer she took for him a basket made of bulrushes, and daubed it with bitumen and pitch; and she put the child in it and placed it among the reeds at the river's brink. And when his sister stood at a distance to know what would be done to him. Now the daughter of Pharoah came down to bathe at the river and her maidens walked beside the river; she saw the basket among the reeds and sent her maid to fetch it. When she opened it she saw the child; and lo, the babe was crying. She took pity on him and said, "This is one of the Hebrews' children" (Exodus 2:1–6).

Moses survived this ordeal, and he later became a leader in the house of Pharoah. He eventually led the people on their exodus journey, and died just before they entered the promised land (Deuteronomy 34).

Herod went after the baby Jesus as soon as he heard from the Magi that they saw a star in the East. The Magi refer to Jesus as a king, a title which is used to again and again throughout the New Testament. In the beginning of the Gospel of John, Nathaniel says of Jesus, "Rabbi, You are the Son of God! You are the King of Israel!" (John 1:49). Later in the same Gospel, Pontius Pilate, the Roman governor of Judea, refers to Jesus as king, although in order to mock Him:

> Pilate entered the praetorium again and called Jesus, and said to Him, "Are you the King of the Jews?" Jesus answered, "Do you say this on your own accord, or did others say it to you about Me? Pilate answered, "Am I a Jew? Your own nation and the chief priests have handed You over to me; what have You done?" Jesus answered, "My kingship is not of this world; if My kingship were of this world, My servants would fight, that I may not be handed over to the Jews; but My kingship is not from this world." Pilate said to Him, "So You are a king? Jesus answered, "You say that I am a king. For this I was born, and for this I have come into the world, to bear witness to the truth. Every one who is of the truth hears My voice." Pilate said to Him, "What is truth?" (John 18:33–38).

Throughout the Scriptures, other people affirm that Jesus is a king, but Jesus never referred to Himself as a king. In his passion narrative, Luke tells us that some from the crowd told Pilate that Jesus called

Himself a king and forbade people from paying tribute to Caesar. This would be considered an act of rebellion, because all Roman citizens had to pay their taxes and honor Caesar as the Roman Emperor (Luke 23:1–5). Yet, Jesus never stirred up a rebellion against the Romans nor did He forbid people to pay their taxes. Actually, the opposite is true; on one occasion, He told His disciples to render unto Caesar what is Caesar's and to God what is God's (Matthew 22:21).

While Jesus never sought political authority and power, He spoke frequently about His Father's kingdom. His parables describing the kingdom of God show a very different kingdom from what people assumed. He used everyday images, such as a mustard seed, yeast and a camel through an eye of a needle, to show that God worked in ways unknown to man. As the prophet Isaiah says, "For my thoughts are not your thoughts, neither are your ways my ways" (Isaiah 55:8). Jesus taught about the kingdom of heaven throughout most of His ministry. Yet, at the end of His life, it is ironic that this peaceful, loving, Jewish carpenter was sentenced to death for the charges of blasphemy and treason, for supposedly calling Himself a king and rebelling against Rome. All four Gospels mention that there was a sign on the cross which read "Jesus King of the Jews," and the Gospel of John emphasizes that this was written in Greek, Latin and Hebrew (John 19:20).

Herod's attempt to kill Jesus' life in the beginning of the Gospel foreshadows what is to come, since at nearly every step, there are opponents of Jesus and His ministry. Throughout the Scriptures, the Pharisees, Scribes and Jewish leaders seek to destroy Jesus and put Him to death: "When the chief priests and the Pharisees heard His parables, they perceived that He was speaking about them. But when they tried to arrest Him, they feared the multitudes, because they held Him to be a prophet" (Matthew 21:45–46). Likewise, even Judas, one of His own disciples, betrays Him, and Peter, His favorite disciple, denies Him three times! So, we should not be surprised that Jesus was in danger even from the very beginning of His life. Yet, Jesus managed to perform many miracles and proclaim the Kingdom of God to the people, and some did hear and accept the Gospel, the same Gospel that is proclaimed to us. Unfortunately, there are still people who do not want the Gospel to grow and, therefore, they try to prevent it from growing. However, the Gospel is continually preached throughout the world and is under the power of God Himself who gives the growth. Our job is to stay out of His way and allow Him to keep planting those seeds of the Kingdom.

CHAPTER TEN

FLIGHT TO EGYPT

MATTHEW 2:13–23

Listen, O heaven! Give ear, O earth!
Let the foundations of the earth be shaken!
Let trembling seize the regions beneath the earth
For our God and creator has clothed Himself in
    created flesh:
He fashioned all creation, yet reveals Himself in
    the womb of her that her formed.
O the depth of the richness of the wisdom and
    knowledge of God!
How incomprehensible are His judgments;
And how unsearchable His ways!
    — *Stikhera for Sixth Hour of the*
    Royal Hours of Christmas

Our family really enjoys traveling. Whether it is a day trip or an extended vacation, we enjoy visiting new places, tasting different foods and learning about new peoples, places and cultures. Even though traveling is not always easy, especially during the present, we still like a good adventure. Very often, the unexpected events are the most cherished, such as the newly discovered local restaurant, or finding the out of the way museum or art gallery. But traveling, especially with children, can also be stressful. You have to pack an extra suitcase for those diapers, bottles, toys and extra baby clothes. We learn from the birth narratives that Jesus also was a world traveler. He had to journey with His family to Egypt when He was very young in order to escape the clutches of King Herod. Immediately following the birth of Jesus, an angel warned Joseph in a dream to take Mary and the newborn baby to Egypt because King Herod wanted to kill Jesus.

Egypt was a very important place in the ancient world. Egypt was home to the great Pyramids, the great Sphinx and the Nile River. Likewise, the Egyptian city of Alexandria was home to one of the best libraries in the world, preserving much of the great Greek and Roman literature. The Egyptian desert was also the home of the monastic movement in the fourth century, when Christians fled the cities in order to live a life of poverty, chastity and obedience in desert communities.[7]

However, Egypt was also the place of exile. In Genesis, we know that Abram and Sarai fled their home and went to Egypt because of the great famine:

> Now there was a famine in the land. So Abram went down to Egypt to sojourn there, for the famine was severe in the land. When he was about to enter Egypt, he said to Sarai, his wife, "I know that you are a woman beautiful to behold; and when the Egyptians see you they will say, "This is his wife; then they will kill me, but they will let you live. Say you are my sister, tha tit may go well with me because of you, and that my life may be spared on your account." When Abram entered Egypt the Egyptians saw that the woman was very beautiful. And when the princess of Pharaoh saw her, they praised her to Pharaoh. And the woman was taken into Pharaoh's house. And for her sake he dwelt well with Abram; and he had sheep, oxen, he-asses, menservants, maidservants, she-asses, and camels (Genesis 12:10–16).

Abram and Sarai eventually left Egypt and returned back to his home, which was near Bethel, one of the first places where Abram spoke with God.

We also know that the baby Moses found himself in Egypt as he was born there and put into the Nile river by his mother. She sent Moses away because Pharoah was angry that the Israelites were multiplying so quickly and he wanted to destroy all of the male children. Thus, his mother sent him away to safety. Ironically, Pharaoh's daughter found the baby Moses and raised him as her own. He eventually became one of the great leaders in Pharoah's household. God used Moses to free the Israelites from their bitter bondage in Egypt.

---

[7] See, for example, Benedicta Ward, *The Sayings of the Desert Fathers* (Kalamazoo, MI: Cistercian Publications, 1975).

Jacob's son Joseph was also in exile in Egypt. He was beaten up by his brothers and left for dead until Midianite traders came by and bought him and sold him to the Ishmaelites who brought Joseph to Egypt:

> Then they sat down to eat; and looking up they saw a caravan of Ishmaelites coming from Gilead, with their camels bearing gum, balm, and myrrh, on their way to carry it down to Egypt. Then Judah said to his brothers, "What profit is it if we slay our brother and conceal his blood? Come, let us sell him to the Ishmaelites, and let not our hand be upon him, for he is our brother, our own flesh." And his brothers heeded him. Then Midianite traders passed by; and they drew Joseph up and lifted him out of the pit, and sold him to the Ishmaelites for twenty shekels of silver; and they took Joseph to Egypt (Genesis 37: 25–28).

Fortunately, even though Joseph was sent to Egypt and served in Potiphar's household, he survived. Joseph was popular because of his ability to interpret dreams.

In the birth narrative, Matthew tells us that Joseph, together with Mary and Jesus, had to flee to Egypt in order to escape the evil clutches of Herod who sought to kill the newborn child. Luckily, God comes to Joseph in a dream telling him to return to his own home since Herod is dead and they will once again be safe:

> But when Herod died behold, an angel of the Lord appeared in a dream to Joseph in Egypt saying, "Rise, take the child and His mother, and go to the land of Israel, for those who sought the child's life are dead." And he rose and took the child and His mother, and went to the land of Israel. But when he heard that Archealaus reigned over Judea in place of his father Herod, he was afraid to go there, and being warned in a dream he withdrew to the district of Galilee. And he went and dwelt in a city called Nazareth, that what was spoken by the prophets might be fulfilled, "He shall be called a Nazarene" (Matthew 2:19–23).

Even in Jesus' infancy His life reads like a cloak and dagger story, fleeing the evil Herod in order to stay alive and then being called back again to His home. Jesus, like Abram, Moses and Joseph, was exiled to Egypt, but God saved Him from the Egyptians. Jesus' exile in Egypt ends with a glimmer of hope as God calls Him out of Egypt to be the Savior of God's people.

CHAPTER ELEVEN

THE CIRCUMCISION AND NAMING
LUKE 2:21

O Most compassionate Lord
While God in essence Thou didst take on
   human likeness without change
And having fulfilled the Law Thou didst accept
   willing circumcision in the flesh
That Thou mightest annul the shadow signs
And remove the veil of our passions
Glory to Thy goodness and compassion
Glory to Thine indescribable condescension,
   O Word.

—Troparion for the Circumcision of our
Lord God and Savior Jesus Christ

On January 1, the Church commemorates the circumcision and naming of Jesus. The Gospel of Luke tells us that eight days following Jesus' birth, He was circumcised and given the name Jesus. Luke's description of this event is short, it is only one sentence, and provides a transition from the birth story to the reception of Jesus in the temple by Symeon: "And at the end of eight days, when He was circumcised, He was called Jesus, the name given by the angel before He was conceived in the womb." Circumcision was performed on all Israelite males as a sign of the covenant between God and Abraham. The outward sign of circumcision was a reminder that God keeps His promises and that the people should obey God:

And God said to Abraham, "As for you, you shall keep My covenant, you and your descendants after you throughout their generations. This is My covenant which you shall keep, between Me and you and your descendants after you: Every male among you shall be circumcised in the flesh of your foreskins, and it shall be a sign of the covenant between me and you. He that is eight days old among you shall be circumcised; every male throughout your generations, whether born in your house or bought with your money from any foreigner who is not of your offspring, both he that bought with you money, shall be circumcised. So shall My covenant be in your flesh an everlasting covenant. Any uncircumcised male who is not circumcised in the flesh of his foreskin shall be cut off from his people; he has broken My covenant" (Genesis 17:9–14. See also Joshua 5:1–9).

While Luke speaks about circumcision of the flesh, there are other references throughout the Scriptures to another circumcision, the circumcision of the heart. Toward the beginning of the book of Deuteronomy, God speaks to Moses about His authority and justice over all His people and speaks about the circumcision of the heart. In ancient Israel, the heart refers not only to the physical organ; the heart is also considered the center of a person:

> Behold, to the Lord your God belong heaven and the heaven of heavens, the earth with all that is in it; yes the Lord set the heart in love upon your fathers and chose their descendants after them; you above all peoples, as of this day. Circumcise therefore the foreskin of your heart, and be no longer stubborn. For the Lord your God is God of gods and Lord of lords, the great, the might, and the terrible God. He executes justice for the fatherless and the widow, and loves the sojourner, giving him food and clothing. Love the sojourner therefore for you were sojourners in the land of Egypt. You shall fear the Lord your God; you shall serve Him and cleave to Him, and by His name you shall swear. He is your praise, He is your God, who has done for you these great and terrible things which your eyes have seen. Your fathers went down to Egypt seven persons; and now the Lord has made you as the stars of heaven for multitude (Deuteronomy 10:12–22. See also Leviticus 26:41).

> For this says the Lord to the men of Judah and to the inhabitants of Jerusalem: Break up your fallow ground, and sow not among thorns. Circumcise yourselves to the Lord, remove the foreskin of your hearts, O men of Judah and inhabitants of Jerusalem; lest My wrath go forth like fire, and burn with none to quench it, because of the evil of your doings (Jeremiah 4:3–4).

While Christians do not have to undergo physical circumcision in order to be members of the body of Christ, an issue which was debated in the epistles of Paul, we instead shall be circumcised of heart.[8]

Also, in this short passage from Luke, Jesus was given His name. In the ancient world, naming generally took place on the eighth day after the birth of a child, and this was equated with accepting the child as one's own; in other words, the child actually came into being when he or she was given their name. Likewise, to have ones' name blotted out or destroyed was as if the person no longer existed: "His roots dry up beneath, and his branches wither above. His memory perishes from the earth and he has no name in the street" (Job 18:17. See also 1 Samuel 24:21, 2 Kings 14:27 and Proverbs 10:7). This is why in the Old Testament there was a strict taboo against profaning the name of the Lord, because in doing so they were profaning the Lord Himself: "You shall not take the name of the Lord your God in vain; for the Lord will not hold him guiltless who takes His name in vain" (Exodus 20:7. See also Leviticus 24:11, Deuteronomy 5:11). Names also referred to one's status or place in the community and society, and the changing of a name meant a change in status or function within the community.

We have numerous examples throughout the Scriptures of name changes. In Genesis 17, God told to His servant Abram that he would be the father of many nations and promised to make His covenant with Abram: "I am the God Almighty, walk before Me, and be blameless. And I will make My covenant between Me and you, and will multiply you exceedingly. Then Abram fell on his face; and God said to him, 'Behold, my covenant is with you, and you shall be the father of a multitude of nations. No longer shall your name be Abram, but your name shall be Abraham; for I have made you the father of a multitude of nations'" (Genesis 17:1–6). Likewise, Abraham's wife had a name change from Sarai to Sarah after she found out that in her old age that she would bear the child Isaac. Jacob's name was changed to Israel after he wrestled with the angel of the Lord (Genesis 32:28). In the New Testament, Saul the Pharisee, who persecuted Christians and assisted with the stoning of Stephen, had his name changed from Saul to Paul (Acts 13:9).

---

[8] See, for example, Paul's letter to the Galatians.

When reading the birth stories, we come to know that Jesus has many names attributed to Jesus, such as Christ (Matthew 1:1), Emmanuel (Matthew 1:23), King of the Jews (Matthew 2:2), Son of the Most High (Luke 1:32), Son of God (Luke 1:35), Savior (Luke 2:11) and Lord (Luke 2:11). We know that Jesus also has other names such as rabbi (John 1:49), Son of Man (Mark 9:31) and son of David (Matthew 9:27).

The Book of Acts shows that the early Christian believers used the name of Jesus to perform miracles and to cast out demons: "But Peter said, 'I have no silver or gold, but I give you what I have; in the name of Jesus Christ of Nazareth, walk'" (Acts 3:6; 4:12. See also Mark 16:17). Furthermore, it was in the name of Jesus that people were baptized for the remission of sins and for entrance into the Christian community. As Peter said to them, "Repent, and be baptized every one of you in the name of Jesus Christ for the forgiveness of your sins; and you shall receive the gift of the Holy Spirit. For the promise is to you and to your children and to all that are far off, every one whom the Lord our God calls him" (Acts 2:38–39). Jesus' name also incurred power and might, even among the demons of this world:

> Have this mind among yourselves, which is yours in Christ Jesus, who, though He was in the form of God, did not count equality with God a thing to be grasped, but emptied Himself, taking the form of a servant, being born in the likeness of men. And being found in human form He humbled Himself and became obedient unto death, even death on a cross. Therefore God has highly exalted Him and bestowed on Him the name which is above every name, that at the name of Jesus every knee should bow, in heaven and on earth and under the earth, and every tongue confess that Jesus Christ is Lord, to the glory of God the Father (Phillipians 2:5–11).

Finally, we know that the early Christian community specifically used Jesus' name in prayer: "Truly, truly, I say to you, if you ask anything of the Father, He will give it to you in My name. Hitherto you have asked nothing in My name, ask, and you will receive, that your joy may be full" (John 16:23–24). Earlier in the same Gospel, Jesus tells His disciples, "Whatever you ask in My name, I will do it, that the Father may be glorified in the Son, if you ask anything in My name, I will do it" (John 14:14). In the Gospel of Matthew, Jesus tells His disciples, "Ask, and it will be given to you; seek, and you shall find; knock, and it will be opened to you. For everyone who asks receives, and he who seeks finds, and to him who knocks it will be opened (Matthew 7:7–8). Furthermore, Jesus Himself gave us the Lord's Prayer which we recite daily and during during the divine services.[9] The Lord's Prayer invokes the name of God as Father:

> Our Father who art in heaven,
> Hallowed be thy name
> Thy kingdom come
> Thy will be done
> On earth as it is in heaven
> Give us this day our daily bread
> And forgive us our debts
> As we also have forgiven our debtors
> And lead us not into temptation,
> But deliver us from evil.
> (Matthew 6:9–13, Luke 11:2–4)

Jesus gave His disciples a powerful statement concerning prayer. A primary role for His followers is to ask or petition the Father. In the Orthodox Christian liturgical tradition, we conclude our prayers with the benediction, "In the name of the Father, and of the Son, and the of the Holy Spirit." Our prayers for the living, for the departed, for the sick and the suffering, for peace, the for the president and congress, and for the military and armed forces are prayed for in the name of Jesus and His Father and the life-giving Spirit. The Apostle Paul says that we are called to pray each and every day: "Pray at all times in the Spirit, with all prayer and supplication. To that end, keep alert with all perseverance, making supplication for all the saints, and also for me, that utterance may be given me in opening my mouth boldly to proclaim the mystery of the Gospel, for which I am an ambassador in chains; that I may declare it boldly, as I ought to speak" (Ephesians 6:18–20).

While Christians are not required to undergo circumcision for religious purposes, we are called to be circumcised of heart, continually living out our life of repentance which we are reminded of at every Church

---

[9] For an excellent reflection on the Lord's Prayer, see Alexander Schmemann, *Our Father* (Crestwood, N.Y.: St. Vladimir's Seminary Press, 2002).

service. Furthermore, our prayer for repentance is always prayed in the name of Jesus Christ, God the Father and the life-giving Spirit. The biblical God makes Himself known to us through His Son Jesus, and therefore, we can call on Him through the name of His Son.

CHAPTER TWELVE

JOHN THE BAPTIST
MATTHEW 3:1–12

> The memory of the righteous is celebrated
>   with songs of praise
> But the Lord's testimony is sufficient for you,
>   O forerunner
> You were shown indeed to be the most
>   honorable of the prophets
> For in the waters you baptize the one whom
>   you preached
> After suffering with joy on behalf of the truth
> You proclaimed even to those in hell
> The God who appeared in the flesh
> Who takes away the sin of the world
> And grants us great mercy.
> — *Troparion for John the Baptist*

In the Scriptures, John is referred to as a "prophet" (Luke 7:26), "the baptist" (Matthew 3:1), the "the greatest born of women" (Luke 7:28) and the "voice crying in the wilderness" (Mark 1:3).[10] John is also known as the "forerunner" since he came before Jesus to prepare the way of repentance:

And this is the testimony of John, when the Jews sent priests and Levites from Jerusalem to ask him, "Who are you?" He confessed, he did not deny, but confessed, "I am not the Christ." And they asked him, "What then? Are you Elijah?" He said, "I am not." "Are you the prophet?" And he answered, "No." They said to him then, "Who are you? Let us have an answer for those who sent to us. What do you say about yourself?" He said, "I am the voice of one crying in the wilder-

---

[10] John is commemorated on January 7 and August 29.

ness, "Make straight the path of the Lord," as the prophet Isaiah said. Now they had been sent from the Pharisee. They asked him, "Then why are you baptizing, if you are neither the Christ, nor Elijah, nor the prophet?" John answered them, "I baptize with water; but among you stands one whom you do not know, even He who comes after me, the thong of whose sandal I am not worthy to unite." This took place in Bethany beyond the Jordan, where John was baptizing (John 1:19–28).

John the baptizer appeared in the wilderness preaching a baptism of repentance for the forgiveness of sins. And there went out to him all the country of Judea, and all the people of Jerusalem; and they were baptized by him in the river Jordan, confessing their sins (Mark 1:4–5. See also Matthew 3:1–12, Luke 3:1–20).

We know that Jesus was not baptized by John, because He needed remission of sins, but so that His baptism would "fulfill all righteousness" (Matthew 3:15). However, while John was clearly baptizing and preaching the Gospel of repentance, some of John's followers thought that he himself was the Christ:

And this is the testimony of John, when the Jews sent priests and Levites from Jerusalem to ask him, "Who are you?" He confessed, he did not deny, but confessed, "I am not the Christ." And they asked him, "What then? Are you Elijah?" He said, "I am not." Are you the prophet?" And he answered, "No." They said to him then, "Who are you? Let us have an answer for those who sent us. What do you say about yourself?" He said, "I am the voice of the one crying in the wilderness, "Make straight the way of the Lord," as the prophet Isaiah said (John 1:19–23).

John was a "voice of one crying in the desert." As a prophet, John called people to repent and turn back to God. John's ministry reminding the Israelites to turn back to God was similar to that of the prophet Isaiah. Isaiah told the Israelites to stop worshipping false gods and turn to the one true living God, the God of Abraham, Isaac and Jacob. However, the Israelites, like us, preferred to worship false gods and idols: "Their land is filled with idols; they bow down to the work of their hands, to what their own fingers have made" (Isaiah 2:8). John appeared as a voice in the wilderness, as another Isaiah, to ultimately prepare the way for Jesus. However, John, like most of the prophets, was persecuted for his preaching:

At that time Herod the tetrarch heard about the fame of Jesus; and he said to his servants, "This is John the Baptist, he has been raised from the dead; that is why these powers are at work in him." For Herod had seized John and bound him and put him in prison, for the sake of Herodias, his brother Philip's wife, because John said to him, "It is not lawful for you to have her." And though he wanted to put him to death, he feared the people, because they held him to be a prophet. But when Herod's birthday came, the daughter of Herodias danced before the company, and pleased Herod, so that he promised an oath to give her whatever she might ask. Prompted by her mother, she said, "Give me the head of John the Baptist here on a platter." And the king was sorry; but because of his oaths and his guests he commanded it to be given; he sent and had John beheaded in the prison, and his head was brought on a platter and given to the girl, and she brought it to her mother. And his disciples came, and took the body and buried it; and they went and told Jesus (Matthew 14:1–12).

John is one of the first martyrs, since his witness to the Gospel of the Kingdom resulted in his death. John came to prepare the way for Jesus even in his own death. Likewise, his life and preaching are a reminder that those who remain faithful to Christ and the Gospel will always be persecuted by the powers and principalities of this world.

CHAPTER THIRTEEN

JORDAN RIVER

MATTHEW 3:1–16

> The waters saw You, O God,
> The waters saw You and were afraid
> For the Cherubim cannot lift their eyes
> Upon Your glory
> Nor can the Seraphim gaze upon You
> But standing by You in fear,
> They first carry You
> And the second glorify Your might.
> With them, O merciful Lord,
> We proclaim Your praises and say:
> O God, who has appeared, have mercy on us.
> — *Apostika for Feast of the Epiphany*

The Jordan River starts at the sea of Galilee, snakes through the vast arid desert of Israel, dividing it lengthwise from east and west, and empties into the Dead Sea. At some places, it is only a few feet deep, and at others, it is very deep and wide. Jesus was baptized in the Jordan River. Jesus' baptism is called the epiphany or theophany, which means "manifestation." It is the manifestation of Jesus to the world and the beginning of his public ministry. This event in the Gospels is celebrated on January 6 and includes the Great Blessing of Water.

Baptism was a common cleansing ritual in the ancient world, symbolizing both renewal and regeneration. The specific location of Jesus' baptism is significant, because in the Old Testament, the Israelites had to cross over the Jordan River in order to get into the promised land. The Jordan is also where the prophet Elisha told Naaman to wash and be cleansed from his leprosy:

After the death of Moses the servant of the Lord, the Lord said to Joshua the son of Nun, Moses' minister, "Moses my servant is dead; now therefore arise, go over this Jordan, you and all this people, into the land which I am giving to them, to the people of Israel. Every place that the sole of your foot will tread upon I have given to you, as I promised to Moses. From the wilderness and this Lebanon as far as the great river, the river Euphrates, all the land of the Hittites to the Great Sea toward the going down of the sun shall be your territory. No man shall be able to stand before you all the days of your life, as I was with Moses so I will be with you; I will not fail or forsake you (Joshua 1:1–2).

Behold, the ark of the covenant of the Lord of all the earth is to pass over before you into the Jordan. Now therefore, take twelve men from the tribes of Israel, from each tribe a man. And when the soles of the feet of the priest who bear the ark of the Lord, the Lord of all the earth, shall rest in the waters of the Jordan, the waters of the Jordan shall be stopped from flowing, and the waters coming down from above shall stand in one heap" (Joshua 3:11–13. See also Joshua 4:8–10 and Psalm 114:3–5).

And Elisha sent a messenger to him, saying, "Go and wash in the Jordan seven times, and your flesh shall be restored, and you shall be clean." But Naaman was angry, and went away, saying, "Behold, I thought that he would surely come out to me, and stand, and call on the name of the Lord his God, and wave his hand over the place, and cure the leper. Are not Abana and Pharpar, the rivers of Damascus, better than all the waters in Israel? Could I not wash in them, and be clean?" So he turned and went away in a rage. But his servants came near and said to him, "My father, if the prophet had commanded you to do some great thing, would you not have done it? How much rather, then, when he says to you, "Wash, and be clean? So he went down and dipped himself seven times in the Jordan, according to the word of the man of God; and his flesh was restored like the flesh of a little child, and he was clean" (2 Kings 5:10–14).

We know from all four Gospels that Jesus came to John to be baptized (Matthew 3:1–16, Mark 1:9–11, Luke 3:21–22, and John 1:31–34). Matthew tells us that John was preaching in the wilderness of Judea and people were coming to him to be baptized. John hesitates to baptize Jesus. As Matthew says, "John would have prevented Him, saying, 'I need to be baptized by you, and do you come to me?'" (Matthew 3:14). However, Jesus consented to be baptized in order to fulfill all righteousness. Matthew tells us that after John baptized Jesus, a voice from heaven said, "This is My beloved Son, with whom I am well pleased" (Matthew 3:17).

This connection between baptism and God's voice or word is very important because baptism is always connected with the preaching of the Gospel. One of the final words from the risen Lord to His disciples was that they should continue His preaching and teaching ministry:

> Now the eleven disciples went to Galilee to the mountain to which Jesus had directed them. And when they saw Him they worshipped Him; but some doubted. And Jesus came and said to them, "All authority in heaven and on earth has been given to Me. Go therefore and make disciples of all nations, baptizing them in the name of the Father, and of the Son and of the Holy Spirit, teaching them to observe all that I have commanded you; and lo, I am with you always, to the close of the age" (Matthew 28:16–20).

In other words, Jesus first taught His disciples and then expected them to go out into the world and preach the good news of the Kingdom, baptizing all nations. Baptism was often a result of the hearing of the good news; people first heard the word of God and then accepted baptism as recalled in the following story about Philip and the Ethiopian eunuch:

> But an angel of the Lord said to Philip, "Rise and go toward the south to the road that goes down from Jerusalem to Gaza." This is a desert road. And he rose and went. And behold, an Ethiopian, a eunuch, a minister of Candace, a queen of the Ethiopians, in charge of all her treasure, had come to Jerusalem to worship and was returning; seated on his chariot, he was reading the prophet Isaiah. And the Spirit said to Philip, "Go up and join this chariot." So Philip ran to him, and heard him reading Isaiah the prophet, and asked, "Do you understand what you are reading?" And he said, "How can I, unless some one guides me?" And he invited Philip to come up; and sit with him. Now the passage of the Scripture which he was reading was this: As a sheep led to the slaughter or a lamb before its shearers is dumb, so he opens not his mouth. In his humiliation justice was denied him. Who can describe his generation? For his life is taken up from the earth." And the eunuch said to Philip, "About whom, pray, does the prophet say this, about himself or about some one else?" then Philip opened his mouth, and beginning with this Scripture he told him the good news of Jesus And as they went along the road they came to some water, and the eunuch said, "See, here is water! What is to prevent my being baptized?

And he commanded the chariot to stop, and they both went down into the water, Philip and the eunuch, and he baptized him. And when they came up out of the water, the Spirit of the Lord caught up Philip; and the eunuch saw him no more, and went on his way rejoicing. But Philip was found at Azotus, and passing on he preached the Gospel to all the towns until he came to Caesarea (Acts 8:26–40).

The eunuch responded to Philip's teaching in faith and was baptized as an affirmation of this faith. Unfortunately, many people today treat baptism as a social or cultural event rather than an entrance into the community of faith. This entrance requires that we accept baptism as a remission of sins but also as entrance into Christ's death. According to the Apostle Paul, baptism is the acceptance of the death of Christ so that we can walk in newness of life:

What shall we say then? Are we to continue in sin that grace may abound? By no means! How can we who died to sin still live in it? Do you not know that all of us who have been baptized into Christ Jesus were baptized into His death? We were buried therefore with Him by baptism into death, so that as Christ was raised from the dead by the glory of the Father, we too may walk in newness of life. For if we have been united with Him in a death like His, we shall certainly be united with Him in a resurrection like His. We know that our old self was crucified with Him so that the sinful body might be destroyed, and we might no longer be enslaved to sin. For He who died is freed from sin. But if we have died with Christ, we believe that we shall also live with Him. For we know that Christ being raised from the dead will never die again; death no longer has dominion over Him. The death He died He died to sin, once for all, but the life He lives He lives to God. So you also must consider yourselves dead to sin and alive to God in Christ Jesus (Romans 6:1–11. See also Colossians 2:9–15, 1 Peter 3:18–22, and Galatians 2:25–28).

We are called to live this new life out in our daily routines of work and family. During the Feast of Epiphany, as we commemorate Jesus' own baptism, we reaffirm our baptism and sanctification as we continue to thank God for all that He has done and continues to do for us. At our baptism, we were given a cross to wear around our necks as a constant reminder of our Christian witness to Christ's own death and resurrection. May we never forget this great gift that has been given to us.

CHAPTER FOURTEEN

THE AXE AT THE ROOT OF THE TREE
MATTHEW 3:10–12

The voice of the Word,
The candlestick of the light
The morning star and the forerunner of the Sun,
Cried in the wilderness to all the people;
Repent and be cleansed while there is yet time
For Christ who delivers the world from corrup-
tion is at hand.
— *Ode 6 Canon of the Feast of Epiphany*

Most people cut their grass easily with a regular lawnmower. However, some patches of land need something much stronger and powerful than a regular lawnmower — a bushwacker. A bushwacker is a large riding mower with a blade so powerful that it can slice rocks, glass and even thin pieces of metal destroying anything that comes in its path. You often see these bushwackers mowing the sides of major highways to clear large parcels of land. It is truly a sight to see someone sitting on this large machine as the blade swirls around and around, cutting everything in its path. For some reason, whenever I see a bushwacker along the side of the road, I think of the prophets.

To me, the prophets were like farmers clearing a field. They came quickly and spoke forcefully on behalf of the Lord. Their preaching leveled everyone and everything in sight, and then they often left as quickly as they came. When reading the prophetic books, you get a sense of immediacy, that an important moment is at hand. I find myself especially returning again and again to the prophets, especially Amos and Hosea. I am not sure why, but their tenor and tone resonate with me, and I find myself drawn to them throughout the year. Perhaps, it is their brevity in speech. Both Amos and Hosea combined are not half the length of the books of Isaiah, Jeremiah or Ezekiel. Amos does not hesitate to begin to prophesy and is very direct as he speaks the word of God to the Israelites:

> The Lord roars from Zion and utters his voice from Jerusalem; the pastures of the shepherds mourn, and the top of Carmel withers. Thus says the Lord, "For three transgressions of Damascus and for four, I will not revoke the punishment; because they have threshed Gilead with the threshing sledges of iron. So I will send a fire upon the house of Hazael, and it shall devour the strongholds of Benhadad. I will break the bar of Damascus, and cut off the inhabitants from the Valley of Aven, and him that holds the scepter from Beth-eden; and the people of Syria shall go into exile to Kir, says the Lord" (Amos 1:2–5).

Amos speaks like this through eight more chapters. He slowly draws the reader in as he describes how God will destroy Israel's neighbors one by one: Damascus, Gaza, Tyre, Edom, and the Ammonites, Moabites, Judahites. However, last but not least, Amos shocks Israel with this final word:

> Thus says the Lord: "For three transgressions of Israel and for four, I will not revoke the punishment; because they sell the righteous for silver and the needy for a pair of shoes-they that trample the head of the poor into the dust of the earth, and turn aside the way of the afflicted; a man and his father go into the same maiden, so that my holy name is profaned; they lay themselves down beside every altar upon garments taken in pledge; and in the house of their God they drink the wine of those who have been fined (Amos 2:6–8).

Amos speaks few words but definitely packs a punch. He waits until he has drawn the reader in and then turns against them! The Israelites are the ones who are oppressing the poor and the impoverished and are not acting according to the Law.

Like Amos, John the Baptist is a prophet who reminds Israel of their sin. He comes to prepare the way of the Lord. He enters quickly in the Gospel narratives. Like most prophets, he is persecuted, and eventually, John is imprisoned and beheaded by Herod Antipas, the son of Herod the Great (Mark 6:16. See also Matthew 14:10 and Luke 9:9).

John's preaching is brief and to the point, and is directed against the leaders of the Jewish people, the Pharisees. John compares the religious leaders to snakes:

> You brood of vipers! Who warned you to flee from the wrath to come? Bear fruit that befits repentance, and not presume to say to yourselves, "We have Abraham as our father; for I tell you, God is able from these stones to raise up children to Abraham. Even now the axe is laid to the root of the trees; every tree therefore that does not bear good fruit is cut down and thrown into the fire. I baptize you with water for repentance, but he who is coming after me is mightier than I, whose sandals I am not worthy to carry; he will baptize you with the Holy Spirit and with fire. His winnowing fork is in his hand, and he will clear his threshing floor and gather his wheat into the granary, but the chaff he will burn with unquenchable fire" (Matthew 3:7–12. See also Isaiah 34:1ff, Jeremiah 8:13ff, Amos 4:9, Habbakuk 3:17–19).

Later, in Matthew's Gospel, Jesus speaks against the Pharisees as He warns them about their hypocrisy:

> Woe to you, scribes and Pharisees, hypocrites! For you build the tombs of the prophets and adorn the monuments of the righteous, saying, "If we have lived in the days of our fathers, we would not have taken part with them in the shedding of blood of the prophets." Thus you witness against yourselves, that you are the sons of those who murdered the prophets. Fill up, then the measure of your fathers. You serpents, you brood of vipers, how are you to escape being sentenced to hell? Therefore I send you prophets and wise men and scribes, some of whom you will kill and crucify, and some you will scourge in your synagogues and persecute from town to town, and upon you may come all the righteous blood shed on earth, from the blood of innocent Abel to the blood of Zechariah the son of Barachiah, whom you murdered between the sanctuary and the altar. Truly, I say to you, all this will come upon this generation (Matthew 23:29–36. See also Matthew 23:1–28).

Jesus speaks in the same vein as John the Baptist, with brief and direct words. Throughout Jesus' preaching ministry, He calls people back to God. The evangelist Mark tells us that the first thing that Jesus did after His baptism was to preach in the region of Galilee saying, "The time is fulfilled, and the Kingdom of God is at hand, repent, and believe in the Gospel" (Mark 1:15). Yet, we know from the Gospel narratives that few people actually chose to listen and to follow. The message of repentance is never a popular message. After all, who wants to change their way of life? John's message is clear; repent because the time is near.

John uses traditional farming imagery to emphasize his point. He says that the axe is laid at the root of the tree, or in other words, the time for judgment is at hand. The choice is either to bear fruit or be ready for the axe. This might seem a bit extreme to modern readers, but John's message is similar to what we find in the prophetic books. We are called to repent, to turn toward God, and to seek to do His will. His will is simple; love Him with all our heart, soul, strength and mind, and love our neighbor as ourself. Jesus says that all the Law and Prophets can be summed up in these two commandments. John and the Apostle Paul both use the image of bearing fruit in relation to this theme of repentance. Paul speaks in his letter to the Galatians about producing fruit of the spirit which he contrasts with the works of the flesh:

> Now the works of the flesh are plain: fornication, impurity, licensiousness, idolatry, sorcery, enmity, strife, jealousy, anger, selfishness, dissension, party spirit, envy, drunkenness, carousing, and the like. I warn you as I warned you before, that those who do such things shall not inherit the kingdom of God. But the fruit of the Spirit is love, joy, peace, patience, kindness, goodness, faithfulness, gentleness, self-control; against such there is not law. And those who belong to Christ Jesus have crucified the flesh with its passions and desires. If we live by the Spirit, let us also walk by the Spirit. Let us have no self-conceit, no provoking of one another, no envy of one another (Galatians 5:19–26).

We need to ask ourselves, are we cultivating fruits of the Spirit? Hopefully, the answer will be a resounding yes! Cultivating fruit is a difficult job, but we are given a lot of help to accomplish this great task. We are given the Scriptures, the liturgical services and prayers of the Church, the example of the saints, and the guidance and direction of our parish priest. If we want to bear fruit, all we need to do is remain open to the Word of God, and it will take root in our heart and bear fruit one day.

CHAPTER FIFTEEN

SYMEON AND ANNA

LUKE 2:22–38

Today Symeon the elder enters the temple rejoic-
ing in spirit,
To receive in his arms Him who gave the law to
Moses
He who Himself now fulfills the law
For Moses was counted worthy to see God
through darkness and sounds not clear.
And his face covered he rebuked the unbeliev-
ing hearts of the Hebrews
But Symeon carried the Pre-Eternal Word of the
Father in bodily form,
And he revealed the Light of the Gentiles, the
Cross and the Resurrection.
Anna was proved to be a prophetess, preaching
the Savior and Deliverer of Israel
Unto Him let us cry aloud
O Christ our God, through the prayers of the
Theotokos have mercy on us.
— *Stikhera on the Litya Feast of the Meeting*
of our Lord and Savior in the Temple

The Church celebrates the feast of the Meeting of the Lord into the
Temple on February 2, forty days following Christmas.[11] The story
behind this feast is recorded in the Gospel of Luke. According to the
Law, a woman had to offer a sacrifice in the temple for her purification
forty days after childbirth. She also had to bring another offering for

---

[11] It is customary in some Orthodox Christian parishes to bless candles on this feast in re-
membrance that Jesus is the light of the world, a theme which is woven throughout the
Gospel narratives, and which is emphasized in the Gospel reading for the feast day.

thanksgiving for the birth of her child. Mary and Joseph's visit to the Temple is similar to Hannah's visit to the Temple after she bore Samuel (I Samuel 1:21).

> The Lord said to Moses, "Say to the people of Israel. If a woman conceives, and bears a male child, then she shall be unclean seven days, as at the time of her menstruation, she shall be unclean. And on the eighth day the flesh of his foreskin shall be circumcised. Then she shall continue for thirty-three days in the blood of her purifying; she shall not touch any hallowed thing, nor come into the sanctuary, until the days of her purifying are completed. But if she bears a female child, then she shall be unclean two weeks, as in menstruation; and she shall continue in the blood of her purifying for sixty-six days. And when the days of her purifying are completed, whether for a son or for a daughter, she shall bring to the priest at the door of the tent of the meeting a lamb a year old for a burnt offering, and a young pigeon or a turtledove for a sin offering and he shall offer it before the Lord and make atonement for her, then she shall be clean from the flow of her blood. This is the law for her who bears a child, either male or female. And if she cannot afford a lamb, then she shall take two turtledoves or two young pigeons, one for a burnt offering and the other for a sin offering; and the priest shall make atonement for her, and she shall be clean (Leviticus 12:1–8. See also Exodus 13:2).

Mary and Joseph fulfilled the Law by bringing Jesus to the Temple along with two turtledoves. These were the sacrifices for those who could not attain a young lamb. At the Temple, they were met by Symeon, who was "righteous and devout, looking for the consolation of Israel, and the Holy Spirit was upon him" (Luke 2:25). Symeon and Anna are only mentioned in Luke's Gospel, so we know nothing more about them other that what Luke tells us. Luke tells us that Anna was a prophetess and the daughter of Phanuel from the tribe of Asher. We do not know who Phanuel was, but the book of Joshua tells us that Asher was the fifth of the twelve tribes listed when the Israelites entered the promised land (Joshua 19:24–31).

When Symeon greeted the Christ child, he offered a prayer to God. We recite or sing St. Symeons' Prayer at every Vespers Service:

> Lord, now lettest Thou Thy servant depart in peace,
> According to Thy word,
> For mine eyes have seen Thy salvation

Which Thou hast prepared in the presence of all peoples,
A light for revelation to the Gentiles,
And for the glory of Thy people Israel.
(Luke 2:29–32)

Symeon's prayer highlights God's salvation, light and glory. These words are seen throughout the birth narratives. Symeon's prayer recalls the prophecies of Isaiah as he awaits the final salvation of God over the enemies of Israel. Isaiah reminds his readers that God redeems us. God sheds His light even on the Gentiles, and on the foreign nations, because all people are subject to Him:

> Thus says God, the Lord, who created the heavens and stretched them out, who spread forth the earth and what comes from it, who gives breath to the people upon it and spirit to those who walk in it; I am the Lord, I have called you in righteousness, I have taken you by the hand and kept you, I have given you as a covenant to the people, a light to the nations, to open the eyes that are blind to bring out the prisoners from the dungeon and from the prison those who sit in darkness. I am the Lord, that is My name; My glory I give to no other, nor My praise to graven images. Behold, the former things have come to pass, the new things I now declare, before thee spring forth, I tell you of them (Isaiah 42:6–9).

> How beautiful are the feet of him who brings good tidings, who publishes peace, who brings good tidings of good, who publishes salvation, who says to Zion, "Your God reigns." Hark your watchmen lift up their voice, together they sing for joy; for eye to eye thee see the return of the Lord to Zion. Break forth together into singing you waste places of Jerusalem; for the Lord has comforted His people, He has redeemed Jerusalem. The Lord has bared His holy arm before the eyes of all the nations; and all the ends of the earth shall see the salvation of our God (Isaiah 52:7–10).

These two passages are found near the end of Isaiah. Earlier, Isaiah says that God finds no redemption in Israel, and predicts the utter destruction of God's people because of their injustice and unrighteousness. However, while Isaiah promises that God will eventually come to judge, He will also bring justice and equity among the peoples. There will be hope again and a new day will dawn: "As one whom his mother comforts, so I will comfort you; you shall be comforted in Jerusalem. You shall see and your heart shall rejoice; your bones shall flourish like the grass; and it shall be known that the hand of the Lord is with His servants, and His indignation is against His enemies" (Isaiah 66:13–16). In this new day, the Gentiles or outsiders will also be welcomed into the house of God. His blessing will be extended to all nations.

In Luke' narrative, Symeon also addresses Jesus' mother Mary and foretells her son's future: "Behold, this child is set for the fall and rising of many in Israel, for a sign that is spoken against (and a sword will pierce through your own soul also), and thoughts out of many hearts will be revealed" (Luke 2:34–35). His words speak of Jesus' crucifixion and Mary's witness to this horrific event (John 19:25–27).

This scene in Luke ends with Anna giving thanks: "And coming up at that very hour she gave thanks to God, and spoke of Him to all who were looking for the redemption of Jerusalem" (Luke 2:38). Joseph and Mary's offering of two turtle doves also symbolized thanksgiving as well as fulfillment of the Law. Likewise, Jesus' circumcision was also a form of thanks, and obedience to the Law.

The feast of the Meeting of the Lord is the culmination of the Christmas season. At the Meeting of the Lord, Jesus enters the temple in Jerusalem, where He is later found teaching and preaching the good news of the Kingdom:

> Now His parents went to Jerusalem every year at the feast of the Passover. And when He was twelve years old, they went up according to custom; and when the feast was ended, as they were returning, the boy Jesus stayed behind in Jerusalem. His parents did not know it, but supposing Him to be in the company they went a day's journey, and they sought Him among their kinsfolk and acquaintances; and when they did not find Him, they returned to Jerusalem, seeking Him. After three days they found Him in the temple, sitting among the teachers, listening to them and asking questions; and all who heard Him were amazed at His understanding and His answers. And when they saw Him they were astonished; and His mother said to Him, "Son, why have You treated us so? Behold, Your father and I have been looking for You anxiously." And He said to them, "How is it that you sought Me?" Did you not know that I must be in My Father's house?" And they did not understand the saying which He spoke to them. And He went down with them and came to Nazareth, and was obedient to them; and His mother kept these things in her heart. And Jesus increased in wisdom and in stature, and in favor with God and man (Luke 2:41–52).

The young Jesus astonishes His teachers with His learning, and throughout the Gospels, He continues to astonish the Pharisees and Saducees in His teaching. They continually try to trap Him in His teaching but always seem to fail. Eventually, they succeed in arresting Him and putting Him on trial, and finally put Jesus to death. However, even at the end of His earthly life, Jesus was obedient to His Father, eventually accepting the cross in order to save us.

SCRIPTURE READINGS FOR THE CHRISTMAS AND EPIPHANY SEASON

ACCORDING TO THE ORTHODOX CHURCH LECTIONARY

CHRISTMAS ROYAL HOURS

First Hour:	Micah 5:2-4, Hebrews 1:1–12, Matthew 1:18–25
Third Hour:	Jeremiah (Baruch) 3:35–4:4, Galatians 3:23-29, Luke 2:1–20
Sixth Hour:	Isaiah 7:10–16, 8:1–4, 9–10; Hebrews 1:10–2:3, Matthew 2:1–12
Ninth Hour:	Isaiah 9:6–7, Hebrews 2:11-18, Matthew 2:13–23

VESPERAL LITURGY OF ST. BASIL THE GREAT (CHRISTMAS EVE DAY)

1. Genesis 1:1-13
2. Numbers 24:2–3, 5–9, 17–18
3. Micah 4:6-7, 5:24
4. Isaiah 11:1–10
5. Jeremiah 3:35–4:4
6. Daniel 2:31–36, 44–45
7. Isaiah 9:6–7
8. Isaiah 7:10–16, 8:1–4, 9–10
9. Galatians 3:15–22 (Epistle)
10. Luke 2:1–20 (Gospel)

ALL NIGHT VIGIL (GREAT COMPLINE & MATINS)

Matthew 1:18–25

DIVINE LITURGY FOR CHRISTMAS DAY

1. Galatians 4:4–7
2. Matthew 2:1–12

CIRCUMCISION OF OUR LORD (JANUARY 1)

1. Genesis 17:1–14
2. Proverbs 8:22–30
3. Proverbs 10:31–11:12
4. John 10:9–16 (Matins Gospel)
5. Colosians 2:8–12 (Divine Liturgy)
6. Luke 2:20–21, 40–52 (Divine Liturgy)

ROYAL HOURS FOR EPIPHANY

First Hour: Isaiah 35:1–10, Acts 13:25–33, Matthew 3:1–11
Third Hour: Isaiah 1:16–20, Acts 19:1–8, Mark 1:1–8
Sixth Hour: Isaiah 12:3–6, Romans 6:3–11, Mark 1:9–15
Ninth Hour: Isaiah 49:8–15, Titus 2:11–14; 3:4–7, Matthew 3:13–17

VESPERAL DIVINE LITURGY OF SAINT BASIL THE GREAT

1. Genesis 1:1–13
2. Exodus 14:15–18, 21–23, 27–29
3. Exodus 15:22–16:1
4. Joshua 3:7–8, 15–17
5. 2 Kings 2:6–14
6. 2 Kings 5:9–14
7. Isaiah 1:16–20
8. Genesis 32:1–10
9. Exodus 2:5–10
10. Judges 6:36–40
11. 1 Kings 18:30–39
12. 2 Kings 2:19–22
13. Isaiah 49:8–15
14. 1 Corinthians 9:19–27
15. Luke 3:1–18

GREAT BLESSING OF WATER

1. Isaiah 35:1–10
2. Isaiah 55:1–13
3. Isaiah 12:3–6
4. 1 Corinthians 10:1–4
5. Mark 1:9–11

DIVINE LITURGY FOR EPIPHANY

1. Titus 2:11–14, 3:4–7
2. Matthew 3:13–17

MEETING OF THE LORD IN THE TEMPLE (FEBRUARY 2)

1. Wisdom 4:6–7:2
2. Isaiah 19:1–5, 12, 16, 19–21
3. Isaiah 6:1–12
4. Luke 2:25–32 (Matins)
5. Hebrews 7:7–17 (Divine Liturgy)
6. Luke 2:22–40 (Divine Liturgy)

PATRISTIC TEXTS FOR THE FEASTS OF CHRISTMAS AND EPIPHANY

G REGORY NAZIANZUS (325–389AD). Gregory was born in Arianzus in Asia Minor in 325, the same year that the council of Nicea took place. His father Gregory was Bishop of Nazianzus, where he raised his two children, Gregory and Nonna. Gregory had a classical education in rhetoric and philosophy and it was during his school years where he befriended Basil, who later became Bishop of Caeseara in Cappadocia. While Gregory did not have an interest in ecclesiastical affairs, he was nonetheless persuaded to be ordained to the diaconate and eventually to the priesthood. Toward the end of his life, he was elevated to the episcopacy and was assigned to the town of Sasima. However, he eventually left his see and returned to his family's estate in Arianzus, where he lived in seclusion for some time. Upon the death of his parents, he sold most of the family estate and distributed it to the poor, living on a small parcel of land. He then retired to a monastery in Seleuci. However, due to numerous theological debates in the Church, Gregory became the bishop of the city of Constantinople during the calling of the Second Ecumenical Council in 381. Gregory wrote numerous theological orations and theological poetry during his lifetime, much of which has been translated into the English language.

Gregory's vocation as a theologian was intimately related with his vocation as a pastor. He was responsible for the physical, spiritual and financial well being of the parishes and communities under his care, but he was also responsible for preserving the Tradition and teachings of the faith, thus, maintaining the catholic and apostolic nature of the Church. Gregory's leadership and guiding principles prevented the

Church from schism and dissention during a difficult period, and thus he is known to be one of the greatest theologians of the fourth century. The selection included is *Oration 38*, which is a sermon on the Nativity of Christ. Gregory's rhetorical style comes through in his words as he reminds his flock that rather than focusing on earthly and material pursuits they should look to the gift of Jesus Christ, the Son of God. Our Christmas canon is based upon his sermon. Gregory is commemorated on January 25.

For Further Reading:

St. Gregory of Nazianzus, *On God and Christ: Five Theological Orations and Two Letters to Cledonius*, translated by Lionel Wickham and Frederick Williams (Crestwood, NY: St. Vladimir's Seminary Press, 2002).

John McGukin, *Saint Gregory of Nazianzus: An Intellectual Biography* (Crestwood, NY: St. Vladimir's Seminary Press, 2001).

Oration 38: On the Birthday or Theophany of Christ

Christ is born, glorify ye Him. Christ from heaven, go ye out to meet Him. Christ on earth; be ye exalted. Sing unto the Lord all the whole earth; and that I may join both in one word, Let the heavens rejoice, and let the earth be glad, for Him Who is of heaven and then of earth. Christ in the flesh, rejoice with trembling and with joy; with trembling because of your sins, with joy because of your hope. Christ of a Virgin; O ye Matrons live as Virgins, that ye may be Mothers of Christ. Who doth not worship Him That is from the beginning? Who doth not glorify Him That is the Last?

Again the darkness is past; again Light is made; again Egypt is punished with darkness; again Israel is enlightened by a pillar. The people that sat in the darkness of ignorance, let it see the Great Light of full knowledge. Old things are passed away, behold all things are become new. The letter gives way, the Spirit comes to the front. The shadows flee away, the Truth comes in upon them. Melchisedec is concluded. He that was without Mother becomes without Father (without Mother of His former state, without Father of His second). The laws of nature are upset; the world above must be filled. Christ commands it, let us not set ourselves against Him. O clap your hands together all ye people, because unto us a Child is born, and a Son given unto us, Whose Government is upon His shoulder (for with the Cross it is raised up), and His Name is called The Angel of the Great Counsel of the Father. Let John cry, Prepare ye the way of the Lord: I too will cry the power of this Day. He Who is not carnal is Incarnate; the Son of God becomes the Son of Man, Jesus Christ the Same yesterday, and to-day, and for ever. Let the Jews be offended, let the Greeks deride; let heretics talk till their tongues ache. Then shall they believe, when they see Him ascending up into heaven; and if not then, yet when they see Him coming out of heaven and sitting as Judge.

Of these on a future occasion; for the present the Festival is the Theophany or Birthday, for it is called both, two titles being given to the one thing. For God was manifested to man by birth. On the one hand Being, and eternally Being, of the Eternal Being, above cause and word, for there was no word before The Word; and on the other hand for our sakes also Becoming, that He Who gives us our being might also give us our Well-being, or rather might restore us by His Incarnation, when we had by wickedness fallen from well being. The name Theophany is given to it in reference to the Manifestation, and that of Birthday in respect of His Birth.

This is our present Festival; it is this which we are celebrating to-day, the Coming of God to Man, that we might go forth, or rather (for this is the more proper expression) that we might go back to God--that putting off the old man, we might put on the New; and that as we died in Adam, so we might live in Christ, being born with Christ and crucified with Him and buried with Him and rising with Him. For I must undergo the beautiful conversion, and as the painful succeeded the more blissful, so must the more blissful come out of the painful. For where sin abounded Grace did much more abound; and if a taste condemned us, how much more doth the Passion of Christ justify us? Therefore let us keep the Feast, not after the manner of a heathen festival, but after a godly sort; not after the way of the world, but in a fashion above the world; not as our own but as belonging to Him Who is ours, or rather as our Master's; not as of weakness, but as of healing; not as of creation, but of re-creation.

And how shall this be? Let us not adorn our porches, nor arrange dances, nor decorate the streets; let us not feast the eye, nor enchant the ear with music, nor enervate the nostrils with perfume, nor prostitute the taste, nor indulge the touch, those roads that are so prone to evil and entrances for sin; let us not be effeminate in clothing soft and flowing, whose beauty consists in its uselessness, nor with the glittering of gems or the sheen of gold or the tricks of colour, belying the beauty of nature, and invented to do despite unto the image of God; Not in rioting and drunkenness, with which are mingled, I know well, chambering and wantonness, since the lessons which evil teachers give are evil; or rather the harvests of worthless seeds are worthless. Let us not set up high beds of leaves, making tabernacles for the belly of what belongs to debauchery. Let us not appraise the bouquet of wines, the kickshaws of cooks, the great expense of unguents. Let not sea and land bring us as a gift their precious dung, for it is thus that I have learnt to estimate luxury; and let us not strive to outdo each other in intemperance (for to my mind every superfluity is intemperance, and all which is beyond absolute need), — and this while others are hungry and in want, who are made of the same clay and in the same manner.

Let us leave all these to the Greeks and to the pomps and festivals of the Greeks, who call by the name of gods beings who rejoice in the reek of sacrifices, and who consistently worship with their belly; evil inventors and worshippers of evil demons. But we, the Object of whose adoration is the Word, if we must in some way have luxury, let us seek it in word, and in the Divine Law, and in histories; especially such as are the origin of this Feast; that our luxury may be akin to and not far removed from Him Who hath called us together. Or do you desire (for to-day I am your entertainer) that I should set before you, my good Guests, the story of these things as abundantly and as nobly as I can, that ye may know how a foreigner can feed the natives of the land, and a rustic the people of the town, and one who cares not for luxury those who delight in it, and one who is poor and homeless those who are eminent for wealth?

One thing connected with the Birth of Christ I would have you hate, the murder of the infants by Herod. Or rather you must venerate this too, the Sacrifice of the same age as Christ, slain before the Offering of the New Victim. If He flees into Egypt, joyfully become a companion of His exile. It is a grand thing to share the exile of the persecuted Christ. If He tarry long in Egypt, call Him out of Egypt by a reverent worship of Him there. Travel without fault through every stage and faculty of the Life of Christ. Be purified; be circumcised; strip off the veil which has covered thee from thy birth. After this teach in the Temple, and drive out the sacrilegious traders. Submit to be stoned if need be, for well I want thou shalt be hidden from those who cast the stones; thou shalt escape even through the midst of them, like God.

If thou be brought before Herod, answer not for the most part. He will respect thy silence more than most people's long speeches. If thou be scourged, ask for what they leave out. Taste gall for the taste's sake; drink vinegar; seek for spittings; accept blows, be crowned with thorns, that is, with the hardness of the godly life; put on the purple robe, take the reed in hand, and receive mock worship from those who mock at the truth; lastly, be crucified with Him, and share His Death and Burial gladly, that thou mayest rise with Him, and be glorified with Him and reign with Him. Look at and be looked at by the Great God, Who in Trinity is worshipped and glorified, and Whom we declare to be now set forth as clearly before you as the chains of our flesh allow, in Jesus Christ our Lord, to Whom be the glory for ever. Amen.

JOHN CHRYSOSTOM (347–407). John was born in Antioch in 347. Like Gregory, John had a classical education that included both rhetoric and philosophy. John studied under the direction of the great philosopher Libanius. When John returned to Antioch, he befriended Bishop Meletius, who baptized John and then ordained him to the diaconate. After baptism, Chrysostom entered the desert for six years. He put himself under the care and guidance of Diodore of Tarsus, the famous Antiochene exegete. Diodore established a school for the learning and interpretation of Scripture and was sought out as one of the greatest teachers of Scripture in the Christian East. His students lived an austere lifestyle devoted to fasting and prayer with the remainder of time devoted to studying Scripture.

Under the new Bishop Flavian, John assisted in assisting the poor and needy, and even though he was a deacon, preached frequently in Church. In 398, John was appointed Bishop in Constantinople, where he found himself at the center of the Roman Empire. While in Constantinople, John had different duties then when he was a priest, yet he still continued to preach and teach as was his custom. As bishop, John's responsibilities were devoted the financial well being of the diocese as well as maintaining peace and concord among the clergy and local parish churches. John was the chief pastor in the capital city and, therefore, had much greater responsibilities then when he was a priest. However, while his obligations took him to various places and locations, John always cared for his community and preached sermons about repentance, love, forgiveness and salvation.

Throughout his ecclesiastical career at Antioch and Constantinople, John devoted himself to preaching the Gospel and ministering to the Church of Christ. Chrysostom encountered a lot of resistance to the truth from the rich upper class of society and the political leaders. However, John's only weapon was the Gospel of Christ, and he used it whenever he had the opportunity. The vast number of his sermons and homilies that survive testify to this fact. John certainly earned the name "golden mouth," and priests and pastors still look to him as an example of as a true pastor of Christ's flock. St. John is commemorated on November 13 and on January 30 together with Basil the Great and Gregory the Theologian.

For Further Reading:

St. John Chrysostom, *On Marriage and Family*, translated by Catherine P. Roth and David Anderson (Crestwood, NY: St. Vladimir's Seminary Press, 1986).

_____. *On Wealth and Poverty* translated by Catherine P. Roth (Crestwood, NY: St. Vladimir's Seminary Press, 1984).

_____. *Six Books on the Priesthood* translated by Graham Neville (Crestwood, NY: St Vladimir's Seminary Press, 1984).

_____. *Baptismal Instructions* translated Paul W. Harkins (Mahwah, NJ: Paulist Press, 1963).

Wendy Mayer and Pauline Allen, *John Chrysostom* (NY: Routledge, 2000).

J. N. D Kelly, *Golden Mouth: The Story of John Chrysostom: Asectic, Preacher, Bishop* (Grand Rapids, MI: Baker Books, 1995).

Homilies on the Gospel of Matthew

HOMILY II

MATT. I. 1. "The book of the generation of Jesus Christ, the Son of David, the Son of Abraham."

Do ye indeed remember the charge, which we lately made you, entreating you to hearken unto all the things that are said with all silence, and mystical quietness? For we are today to set foot within the holy vestibule, wherefore I have also put you in mind of the charge.

Since, if the Jews, when they were to approach "a mountain that burned, and fire, and blackness, and darkness, and tempest;"--or rather when they were not so much as to approach, but both to see and to hear these things from afar;--were commanded for three days before to abstain from their wives, and to wash their garments, and were in trembling and fear, both themselves and Moses with them; much more we, when we are to hearken to such words, and are not to stand far from a smoking mountain, but to enter into Heaven itself, ought to show forth a greater self-denial ;not washing our garments, but wiping clean the robe of our soul, and ridding ourselves of all mixture with worldly things. For it is not blackness that ye shall see, nor smoke, nor tempest, but the King Himself sitting on the throne of that unspeakable glory, and angels, and archangels standing by Him, and the tribes of the saints, with those interminable myriads.

For such is the city of God, having "the Church of the first-born, the spirits of the just, the general assembly of the angels, the blood of sprinkling "whereby all are knit into one, and Heaven hath received the things of earth, and earth the things of Heaven, and that peace hath come which was of old longed for both by angels and by saints.

Herein standeth the trophy of the cross, glorious, and conspicuous, the spoils won by Christ, the first-fruits of our nature, the booty of our King; all these, I say, we shall out of the Gospels know perfectly. If thou follow in becoming quietness, we shall be able to lead thee about everywhere, and to show where death is set forth crucified, and where sin is hanged up, and where are the many and wondrous offerings from this war, from this battle.

Thou shalt see likewise the tyrant here bound, and the multitude of the captives following, and the citadel from which that unholy demon overran all things in time past. Thou wilt see the hiding places, and the dens of the robber, broken up now, and laid open, for even there also was our King present.

But be not thou weary, beloved, for if any one were describing a visible war, and trophies, and victories, wouldest thou feel no satiety at all; nay, thou wouldest not prefer either drink or meat to this history. But if that kind of narrative be welcome, much more this. For consider what a thing it is to hear, how on the one side God from Heaven, arising "out of the royal thrones, leaped down "unto the earth, and even unto hell itself, and stood in the battle array; and how the devil on the other hand set himself in array against Him; or rather not against God unveiled, but God hidden in man's nature.

And what is marvellous, thou wilt see death destroyed by death, and curse extinguished by curse, and the dominion of the devil put down by those very things whereby he did prevail. Let us therefore rouse ourselves thoroughly, and let us not sleep, for lo, I see the gates opening to us; but let us enter in with all seemly order, and with trembling, setting foot straightway within the vestibule itself.

But what is this vestibule? "The book of the generation of Jesus Christ, Son of David, Son of Abraham." "What sayest thou? Didst thou not promise to discourse of the Only-begotten Son of God, and dost thou make mention of David, a man born after a thousand generations, and say that he is both father and ancestor?" Stay, seek not to learn all at once, but gently and by little and little. Why, it is in the vestibule that thou art standing, by the very porch; why then dost thou hasten towards the inner shrine? As yet thou hast not well marked all without. For neither for a while do I declare unto thee that other generation: or rather not even this which cometh after, for it is unutterable, and unspeakable. And before me the Prophet Esaias hath told thee this; where when proclaiming His passion, and His great care for the world, and admiring who He was, and what He became, and whither He descended, he cried out loud and clear, saying thus, "Who shall declare His generation?"

It is not then of that we are now to speak, but of this beneath, this which took place on earth, which was amongst ten thousand witnesses. And concerning this again we will relate in such wise as it may be possible for us, having received the grace of the Spirit. For not even this may any one set forth altogether plainly, forasmuch as this too is most awful. Think not, therefore, it is of small things thou art hearing, when thou hearest of this birth, but rouse up thy mind, and straightway tremble, being told that God hath come upon earth. For so marvellous was this, and beyond expectation, that because of these things the very angels formed a choir, and in behalf of the world offered up their praise for them, and the prophets from the first were amazed at this, that "He was seen upon earth, and conversed with men." Yea, for it is far beyond all thought to hear that God the Unspeakable, the Unutterable, the Incomprehensible, and He that is equal to the Father, hath passed through a virgin's womb, and hath vouchsafed to be born of a woman, and to have Abraham and David for forefathers. But why do I say Abraham and David? For what is even more amazing, there are those women, whom we have lately mentioned.

Hearing these things, arise, and surmise nothing low: but even because of this very thing most of all shouldest thou marvel, that being Son of the Unoriginate God, and His true Son, He suffered Himself to be called also Son of David, that He might make thee Son of God. He suffered a slave to be father to Him, that He might make the Lord Father to thee a slave.

Seest thou at once from the beginning of what nature are the Gospels? If thou doubt concerning the things that pertain to thee from what belongs to Him believe these also For it is far more difficult, judging by human reason, for God to become man, than for a man to be declared a Son of God. When therefore thou art told that the Son of God is Son of David and of Abraham, doubt not any more that thou too, the son of Adam, shall be son of God. For not at random, nor in vain did He abase Himself so greatly, only He was minded to exalt us. Thus He was born after the flesh, that thou mightest be born after the Spirit; He was born of a woman, that thou mightest cease to be the son of a woman.

Wherefore the birth was twofold, both made like unto us, and also surpassing ours. For to be born of a woman indeed was our lot, but "to be born not of blood, nor of the will of flesh, nor of man," but of the Holy Ghost, was to proclaim beforehand the birth surpassing us, the birth to come, which He was about freely to give us of the Spirit. And everything else too was like this. Thus His baptism also was of the same kind, for it partook of the old, and it partook also of the new. To be baptized by the prophet marked the old, but the coming down of the Spirit shadowed out the new. And like as though any one were to place himself in the space between any two persons that were standing apart, and stretching forth both his hands were to lay hold on either side, and tie them together; even so hath He done, joining the old covenant with the new, God's nature with man's, the things that are His with ours.

Seest thou the flashing brightness of the city, with how great a splendor it hath dazzled thee from the very beginning? how it hath straightway shown the King in thine own form; as though in a camp? For neither there doth the king always appear bearing his proper dignity, but laying aside the purple and the diadem, he often disguises himself in the garb of a common soldier. But there it is, lest by being known he should draw the enemy upon himself; but here on the contrary, lest, if He were known, He should cause the enemy to fly from the conflict with Him, and lest He should confound all His own people: for His purpose was to save, not to dismay.

For this reason he hath also straightway called Him by this title, naming Him Jesus. For this name, Jesus, is not Greek, but in the Hebrew language it is thus called Jesus; which is, when interpreted into the Greek tongue, "A Saviour." And He is called a Saviour, from His saving His people.

Seest thou how he hath given wings to the hearer, at once speaking things familiar, and at the same time by these indicating to us things beyond all hope? I mean that both these names were well known to the Jews. For, because the things that were to happen were beyond expectation, the types even of the names went before, in order that from the very first all the unsettling power of novelty might be taken away. Thus he is called Jesus, who after Moses brought the people into the land of promise. Hast thou seen the type? Behold the truth. That led into the land of promise, this into heaven, and to the good things in the heavens; that, after Moses was dead, this after the law had ceased; that as a leader, this as a King.

However, lest having heard the word Jesus, thou shouldest by reason of the identity of the name be perplexed, he hath added, "Jesus Christ, Son of David." But that other was not of David, but of another tribe.

But wherefore doth he call it a "book of the generation of Jesus Christ," while yet this book hath not the birth only, but the whole dispensation? Because this is the sum of the whole dispensation, and is made an origin and root of all our blessings. As then Moses calleth it the book of heaven and earth, although he hath not discoursed of heaven and earth only, but also of all things that are in the midst thereof; so also this man hath named his book from that which is the sum of all the great things done. For that which teems with astonishment, and is beyond hope and all expectation, is that God should become man. But this having come to pass, all afterwards follows in reasonable consequence.

But wherefore did he not say, "the Son of Abraham," and then "the Son of David?" it is not, as some suppose, that he means to proceed upward from the lower point, since then he would have done the same as Luke, but now he doth the contrary. Why then hath he made mention of David? The man was in the mouths of all, both from his distinction, and from the time, for he had not been so very long since dead, like Abraham. And though God made promises to both, yet the one, as old, was passed over in silence, while the other, as fresh and recent, was repeated of all. Themselves, for instance, say, "Doth not Christ come of the seed of David, and out of Bethlehem, the town where David was?" And no man called Him Son of Abraham, but all Son of David; and that because this last was more in the recollection of all, both on account of the time, as I have already said, and because of his royalty. On this principle again all the kings whom they had in honor after his time were named from him, both by the people themselves and by God. For both Ezekiel and other prophets besides speak of David as coming and rising again; not meaning him that was dead, but them who were emulating his virtue. And to Hezekiah He saith, "I will defend this city, for mine own sake and for my servant David's sake." And to Solomon too He said, that for

David's sake He rent not the kingdom during his lifetime. For great was the glory of the man, both with God and with men.

On account of this he makes the beginning at once from him who was more known, and then runs up to his father; accounting it superfluous, as far as regards the Jews, to carry the genealogy higher up. For these were principally the persons held in admiration; the one as a prophet and a king, the other as a patriarch and a prophet.

"But whence is it manifest that He is of David?" one may say. For if He was not sprung of a man, but from a woman only, and the Virgin hath not her genealogy traced, how shall we know that He was of David's race? Thus, there are two things inquired; both why His mother's genealogy is not recited, and wherefore it can be that Joseph is mentioned by them, who hath no part in the birth: since the latter seems to be superfluous, and the former a defect.

Of which then is it necessary to speak first? How the Virgin is of David. How then shall we know that she is of David? Hearken unto God, telling Gabriel to go unto "a virgin betrothed to a man (whose name was Joseph), of the house and lineage of David." What now wouldest thou have plainer than this, when thou hast heard that the Virgin was of the house and lineage of David?

Hence it is evident that Joseph also was of the same. Yes, for there was a law, which bade that it should not be lawful to take a wife from any other stock, but from the same tribe. And the patriarch Jacob also foretold that He should arise out of the tribe of Judah, saying on this wise: "there shall not fail a ruler out of Judah, nor a governor out of his loins, until He come for whom it is appointed, and He is the expectation of the Gentiles."

"Well; this prophecy doth indeed make it clear that He was of the tribe of Judah, but not also that He was of the family of David. Was there then in the tribe of Judah one family only, even that of David, or were there not also many others? And might it not happen for one to be of the tribe of Judah, but not also of the family of David?"

Nay, lest thou shouldest say this, the evangelist hath removed this suspicion of thine, by saying, that He was "of the house and lineage of David."

And if thou wish to learn this from another reason besides, neither shall we be at a loss for another proof. For not only was it not allowed to take a wife out of another tribe, but not even from another lineage, that is, from another kindred. So that if either we connect with the Virgin the words, "of the house and lineage of David," what hath been said stands good; or if with Joseph, by that fact this also is proved. For if Joseph was of the house and lineage of David, he would not have taken his wife from another than that whence he himself was sprung.

"What then," one may say, "if he transgressed the law?" Why, for this cause he hath by anticipation testified that Joseph was righteous, on purpose that thou mightest not say this, but having been told his virtue, mightest be sure also that he would not have transgressed the law. For he who was so benevolent, and free from passion, as not to wish, even when urged by suspicion, to attempt inflicting punishment on the Virgin, how should he have transgressed the law for lust? he that showed wisdom and self-restraint beyond the law (for to put her away, and that privily, was to act with self-restraint beyond the law), how should he have done anything contrary to the law; and this when there was no cause to urge him?

Now that the Virgin was of the race of David is indeed from these things evident; but wherefore he gave not her genealogy, but Joseph's, requires explanation. For what cause was it then? It was not the law among the Jews that the genealogy of women should be traced. In order then that he might keep the custom, and not seem to be making alterations from the beginning, and yet might make the Virgin known to us, for this cause he hath passed over her ancestors in silence, and traced the genealogy of Joseph. For if he had done this with respect to the Virgin, he would have seemed to be introducing novelties; and if he had passed over Joseph in silence, we should not have known the Virgin's forefathers. In order therefore that we might learn, touching Mary, who she was, and of what origin, and that the laws might remain undisturbed, he hath traced the genealogy of her espoused husband, and shown him to be of the house of David. For when this hath been clearly proved, that other fact is demonstrated with it, namely, that the Virgin likewise is sprung from thence, by reason that this righteous man, even as I have already said, would not have endured to take a wife from another race.

There is also another reason, which one might mention, of a more mystical nature, because of which the Virgin's forefathers were passed over in silence; but this it were not seasonable now to declare, because so much has been already said.

Wherefore let us stay at this point our discourse concerning the questions, and in the meanwhile let us retain with accuracy what hath been revealed to us; as, for instance, why he mentioned David first; wherefore he called the book, "a book of the generation;" on what account he said, "of Jesus Christ;" how the birth is common and not common; whence it was that Mary was shown to be from David; and wherefore Joseph's genealogy is traced, while her ancestors are passed over in silence.

For if ye retain these things, ye will the more encourage us with respect to what is to come; but if ye reject and cast them from your mind, we shall be the more backward as to the rest Just as no husbandman would care to pay attention to a soil which had destroyed the former seed.

Wherefore I entreat you to revolve these things. For from taking thought concerning such matters, there springs in the soul some great good, tending unto salvation. For by these meditations we shall be able to please God Himself; and our mouths will be pure from insults, and filthy talking, and reviling, while they are exercising themselves in spiritual sayings; and we shall be formidable to the devils, while arming our tongue with such words; and we shall draw unto ourselves God's grace the more, and it will render our eye more piercing. For indeed both eyes and mouth and hearing He set in us to this intent, that all our members may serve Him, that we may speak His words, and do His deeds, that we may sing unto Him continual hymns, that we may offer up sacrifices of thanksgiving, and by these may thoroughly purify our consciences.

For as a body will be more in health when enjoying the benefits of a pure air, even so will a soul be more endued with practical wisdom when nourished in such exercises as these. Seest thou not even the eyes of the body, that when they abide in smoke they are always weeping; but when they are in clear air, and in a meadow, and in fountains and gardens. they become more quick sighted and more healthy? Like this is the soul's eye also, for should it feed in the meadow of spiritual oracles, it will be clear and piercing, and quick of sight; but should it depart into the smoke of the things of this life, it will weep without end, and wail both now and hereafter. For indeed the things of this life are like smoke. On this account also one hath said, "My days have failed like smoke." He indeed was referring to their shortness of duration, and to their unsubstantial nature, but I would say that we should take what is said, not in this sense alone, but also as to their turbid character.

For nothing doth so hurt and dim the eye of the soul as the crowd of worldly anxieties and the swarm of desires. For these are the wood that feedeth this smoke. And as fire, when it lays hold of any damp and saturated fuel, kindles much smoke; so likewise this desire, so vehement and burning, when it lays hold of a soul that is (so to speak) damp and dissolute, produces also in its way abundance of smoke. For this cause there is need of the dew of the Spirit, and of that air, that it may extinguish the fire, and scatter the smoke, and give wings to our thoughts. For it cannot, it cannot be that one weighed down with so great evils should soar up to heaven; it is well if being without impediment we can cleave our way thither; or rather it is not possible even so, unless we obtain the wing of the Spirit. Now if there be need both of an unencumbered mind, and of spiritual grace, that we may mount up to that height; what if there be none of these things, but we draw to ourselves whatever is opposite to them, even a satanical weight? how shall we be able to soar upwards, when dragged down by so great a load? For indeed, should any one attempt to weigh our words as it were in just balances; in ten thousand talents of worldly talk he will scarcely find an hundred pence of spiritual words, or rather, I should say, not even ten farthings. Is it not then a disgrace, and an extreme mockery, that if we have a servant, we make use of him for the most part in things necessary, but being possessed of a tongue, we do not deal with our member so well even as with a slave, but on the contrary make use of it for things unprofitable, and mere makeweights? And would it were only for make weights: but now it is for what are contrary and hurtful and in no respect advantageous to us. For if the things that we spoke were profitable to us, they would assuredly be also pleasing to God. But as it is, whatever the devil may suggest, we speak it all, now laughing, and now speaking wittily; now cursing and insulting, and now swearing, lying, and taking false oaths; now murmuring, and now making vain babblings, and talking trifles more than old wives; uttering all things that are of no concern to us.

For, tell me, who of you that stand here, if he were required, could repeat one Psalm, or any other portion of the divine Scriptures? There is not one.

And it is not this only that is the grievous thing, but that while ye are become so backward with respect to things spiritual, yet in regard of what belongs to Satan ye are more vehement than fire. Thus should any one be minded to ask of you songs of devils and impure effeminate melodies, he will find many that know these perfectly, and repeat them with much pleasure.

But what is the answer to these charges? "I am not," you will say, "one of the monks, but I have both a wife and children, and the care of a household." Why, this is what hath ruined all, your supposing that the reading of the divine Scriptures appertains to those only, when ye need it much more than they. For they that dwell in the world, and each day receive wounds, these have most need of medicines. So that it is far worse than not reading, to account the thing even "superfluous:" for these are the words of diabolical invention. Hear ye not Paul saying, "that all these things are written for our admonition"?

And thou, if thou hadst to take up a Gospel, wouldest not choose to do so with hands unwashed; but the things that are laid up within it, dost thou not think to be highly necessary? It is because of this, that all things are turned upside down.

For if thou wouldest learn how great is the profit of the Scriptures, examine thyself, what thou becomest by hearing Psalms, and what by listening to a song of Satan; and how thou art disposed when staying in a Church, and how when sitting in a theatre; and thou wilt see that great is the difference between this soul and that, although both be one. Therefore Paul said, "Evil communications corrupt good manners." For this cause we have need continually of those songs, which serve as charms from the Spirit. Yes, for this it is whereby we excel the irrational creatures, since with respect to all other things, we are even exceedingly inferior to them.

This is a soul's food, this its ornament, this its security; even as not to hear is famine and wasting; for "I will give them," saith He, "not a famine of bread, nor a thirst of water, but a famine of hearing the word of the Lord."

What then can be more wretched? When the very evil, which God threatens in the way of punishment, this thou art drawing upon thine head of thine own accord, bringing into thy soul a sort of grievous famine, and making it the feeblest thing in the world? For it is its nature both to be wasted and to be saved by words. Yea, this leads it on to anger; and the same kind of thing again makes it meek: a filthy expression is wont to kindle it to lust, and it is trained to temperance by speech full of gravity.

But if a word merely have such great power, tell me, how is it thou dost despise the Scriptures? And if an admonition can do such great things, far more when the admonitions are with the Spirit. Yes, for a word from the divine Scriptures, made to sound in the ear, doth more than fire soften the hardened soul, and renders it fit for all good things.

In this way too did Paul, when he had found the Corinthians puffed up and inflamed, compose them, and make them more considerate. For they were priding themselves on those very things, touching which they ought to have been ashamed, and to have hid their face. But after they had received the letter, hear the change in them, of which the Teacher himself hath borne witness for them, saying on this wise: for "this very thing, that ye sorrowed after a godly sort, what carefulness it wrought in you, yea, what clearing of yourselves, yea, what indignation, yea, what zeal, yea, what revenge." In this way do we bring to order servants and children, wives, and friends, and make our enemies friends.

In this way the great men too, they that were dear to God, became better. David, for instance, after his sin, when he had had the benefit of certain words, then it was that he came unto that most excellent repentance; and the apostles also by this mean became what they did become, and drew after them the whole world.

"And what is the profit," one may say, "when any one hears, but doeth not what is said?" No little will the profit be even from hearing. For he will go on to condemn himself, and to groan inwardly, and will come in time also to do the things that are spoken of. But he that doth not even know that he hath sinned, when will he cease from his negligence? When will he condemn himself?

Let us not therefore despise the hearing of the divine Scriptures. For this is of Satan's devising; not suffering us to see the treasure, lest we should gain the riches. Therefore he saith that the hearing the divine laws is nothing, lest he should see us from the hearing acquiring the practice also.

Knowing then this his evil art, let us fortify ourselves against him on all sides, that being fenced with this armor, we may both abide unconquered ourselves, and smite him on the head: and thus, having crowned ourselves with the glorious wreaths of victory, we may attain unto the good things to come, by the grace and love towards man of our Lord Jesus Christ, to whom be glory and might for ever and ever. Amen.

EPHREM THE SYRIAN (306–373). Ephrem was born in Nisbis (modern day Syria) and raised in a pagan household, but was eventually baptized by Bishop James of Nisbis at the age of 18. Later Ephrem went to live in Edessa (modern day Iraq) where he was ordained a deacon. As a deacon he was given permission to preach and from later writers we know that he was considered a very good preacher. Ephrem was never ordained to the priesthood, but this did not prevent him from fulfilling his ministry in the Church. Ephrem was an avid writer and wrote numerous hymns on liturgical feasts in the Church year as well as full commentaries on books of scripture. The two selections included from Ephrem are hymns on the Nativity and on Epiphany (Theophany). These hymns were used in a liturgical setting and therefore are quite different than a sermon or homily. Ephrem is commemorated on January 28.

For Further Reading:

Ephrem the Syrian, *Hymns on Paradise,* translated by Sebastian Brock (Crestwood, NY: St. Vladimir's Seminary Press, 1990).

Ephrem the Syrian, *Hymns,* translated by Kathleen McVey (Mahwah, NJ: Paulist Press, 1989).

1. Christ and chrism are conjoined; the secret with the visible is mingled: the chrism anoints visibly, — Christ seals secretly, the lambs newborn and spiritual, the prize of His twofold victory; for He engendered it of the chrism, and He gave it birth of the water.

2. How exalted are your Orders! For she that was a sinner anointed, as a handmaid, the feet of her Lord. But for you, as though His minister, Christ by the hand of His servants, seals and anoints your bodies. It befits Him the Lord of the flock, that in His own person He seal His sheep.

3. Since then she, that sinner, stood in need of forgiveness, the anointing was for her an offering, and by it her love reconciled her Lord. But you who are the flock, among the profane and unbelievers, the Truth by the chrism is your seal, to separate you from the strayed.

4. From the peoples he separated the People, by the former seal of circumcision; but by the seal of anointing, the peoples He separates from the People. When the peoples were in error, the People He separated from the peoples; now when the People has erred from Him, He separates the peoples from thence.

5. Of the dust of the pure soil, Naaman bore away and returned to his place; that he by this holy dust, might be separated and known from the unclean. The chrism of Christ separates, the sons of the mystery from strangers: and by it they that are within are separated, and known from them that are without.

6. The oil which Elijah multiplied, might be tasted with the mouth; for the cruse was that of the widow, it was not that of the chrism. The oil of our Lord that is in the cruse, it is not food for the mouth: the sinner that was a wolf without, it makes him a lamb in the flock.

7. The chrism of the meek and lowly One, changes the stubborn to be like its Lord. The Gentiles were wolves and feared, the severe rod of Moses. Lo! the chrism seals them and makes, a flock of sheep out of the wolves! And the wolves that had fled from the rod, lo! they have taken refuge in the Cross!

8. The leaf of olive arrived, brought as a figure of the anointing; the sons of the Ark rejoiced to greet it, for it bore good tidings of deliverance. Thus also ye rejoiced to greet it, even this holy anointing. The bodies of sinners were glad in it, for it brought good tidings of deliverance.

9. The oil again that Jacob poured, upon the stone when he sealed it, that it should be between him and God, and that he might offer there his tithes; lo! in it is a symbol of your bodies, how by chrism they are sealed as holy, and become temples for God, where He shall be served by your sacrifices.

10. When Moses had sealed and anointed, the sons of Aaron the Levite, the fire consumed their bodies; the fire spared their vestments. But ye my brethren blessed are ye, for the fire of grace has come down, has consumed utterly your offences, and cleansed and hallowed your bodies!

11. As for the anointing of Aaron my brethren, it was the vile blood of beasts, that it sprinkled in the horns of the altar. The anointing of truth is this; wherein the living and all-lifegiving Blood, is sprinkled inwardly in your bodies. is mingled in your understandings, is infused through your inmost chambers.

12. The anointed priests used to offer, the slain bodies of beasts; Ye, O anointed and excelling, your offerings are your own bodies. The anointed Levites offered, the inward parts taken, from beasts: ye have excelled the Levites, for your hearts ye have Consecrated.

13. The anointing of the People was--a foreshadowing of Christ; their rod a mystery of the Cross; their lamb a type of the Only begotten; their tabernacle a mystery of your Churches; their circumcision a sign of your sealing. Under the shadow of your goodly thing, sat the People of old.

14. Thus the truth is likened, to a great shadowing tree: it cast its shade on the People; it struck its root among the peoples. The People abode under its shadows, whose shadows were its mysteries; but the Gentiles lodged on its bough, and plucked and ate of its fruits.

15. As for the anointing of Saul to be king; the sweeter was its saviour, so much fouler was the saviour of his heart. The Spirit struck him and fled. Your anointing which ye have is greater; for your minds are censers, in your temples the Spirit exults, a chamber forever shall ye be unto Him.

16. As for the anointing of David my brethren; the Spirit came down and made sweet saviour, in the heart of the man wherein He delighted; the saviour of his heart was as the saviour of his action. The Spirit dwelt

in him and made song in him. Your anointing which ye have is greater, for Father and Son and Holy Ghost, have moved and come down to dwell in you.

17. When the leper of old was cleansed, the priest used to seal him with oil, and to lead him to the waterspring. The type has passed and the truth is come; lo! with chrism have ye been sealed, in baptism ye are perfected, in the flock ye are intermixed, from the Body ye are nourished.

18. What leper when he has been cleansed, turns again and desires his leprosy? Ye have put off transgressions — forsake it! None puts on the leprosy he had put off. It has fallen and sunk — let it not be drawn out! It is wasted and worn — let it not be renewed! Let not corruption come out upon you, whom the chrism of Christ has anointed!

19. The vessel moulded of clay, gains beauty from the water, receives strength from the fire; but if it slips it is ruined, it cannot be afresh renewed. Ye are vessels of grace; be ye ware of it, even of justice, for it grants not two renewals.

20. How like are ye in comparison, with the Prophet whom the fish yielded up! The Devourer has given you back for he was constrained, by the Power Which constrained the fish. Jonah was for you as a mirror, since not again did the fish swallow him, let not again the Devourer swallow you: being yielded up be ye like Jonah!

21. Goodly ointment on the head of our Lord did Mary pour; its saviour was fragrant through all the house. Likewise the saviour of your anointing, has been fragrant and perfumed the heavens, to the Watchers on high; doing pleasure to Satan its saviour is overpowering; to God its odour is sweet.

22. The crowds in the desert were like unto sheep that have no shepherd. The Merciful became their shepherd, and multiplied to them the pasture of bread. Yea, blessed are ye that are perfect, that are sealed as lambs of Christ, that of His Body and Blood are made worthy; the Pastor Himself is become pasture for you!

23. Out of water He made the wine, He gave it for drink to the youths in the feast. For you who are keeping the fast, better is the unction than drink. In His wine the betrothed are wedded, by His oil the wedded are sanctified. By His wine is union; by His oil sanctification.

24. The sheep of Christ leaped for joy, to receive the seal of life, that ensign of kings which has ever put sin to flight. The Wicked by Thy ensign is routed, iniquities by Thy sign are scattered. Come, ye sheep, receive your seal, which puts to flight them that devour you!

25. Come, ye lambs, receive your seal, for it is truth that is your seal! This is the seal that separates, them of the household from strangers. The steel circumcised alike, the gainsayers and the sons of Hagar. If circumcision be the sign of the sheep, lo! by it the goats are signed.

26. But ye, who are the new flock, have put off the doings of wolves, and as lambs are made like to the Lamb. One by changing has changed all; the Lamb to the wolves gave Himself to be slain; the wolves rushed and devoured Him and became lambs; for the Shepherd was changed into a Lamb; likewise the wolf forgot his nature.

27. Look on me also in Thy mercy! be not branded on me the seal, of the goats the sons of the left hand! let not Thy sheep become a goat! For though to justify myself I sufficed not, yet to be a sinner I willed not. Turn thine eyes, O my Lord, from what I have done, and seek not only what I have willed.

28. From them that write and them that preach, from them that hear and them that are sealed, let glory go up to Christ, and through Him to His Father be exaltation! He Who gives words to them that speak, and gives voice to them that preach, has given understanding to them that hear, and consecrates chrism for him that is sealed.

BIBLIOGRAPHY

COMMENTARIES ON THE BIRTH NARRATIVES AND CHRISTMAS SEASON

Brown, Raymond E. *An Adult Christ at Christmas*. Collegeville, MN: The Liturgical Press, 1978.

_____. *Birth of the Messiah*. NY: Doubleday, 1977.

Department of Religious Education. *The Services of Christmas: The Nativity of our Lord God and Savior Jesus Christ*. Syosset, NY: Orthodox Church in America, 1981.

Dunlop, Olga. *Living God: A Catechism Volume 1*. Crestwood, NY: St. Vladimir's Seminary Press, 1996.

Hopko, Thomas. *The Winter Pascha*. Crestwood, NY: St. Vladimir's Seminary Press, 1984.

Talley, Thomas. *Origins of the Liturgical Year*. Collegeville, MN: The Liturgical Press, 1986.

PATRISTIC TEXTS

Augustine of Hippo. *Sermons to the People: Advent, Christmas, New Year's, and Epiphany*. Trans. and edited by William Griffin. NY: Random House, 2002.

Emphrem the Syrian. *Hymns*. Trans. and edited Kathleen E. McVey. Mahwah, NJ: Paulist Press, 1989.

Gregory Nazianzen. *Select Orations*. (Edited) Philip Schaff Nicene and Post-Nicene Fathers Volume 7 Grand Rapids, MI: Wm. B. Eerdmans Publishing, 1983.

John Chrysostom. *Homilies on St. Matthew*. Edited Philip Schaff Nicene and Post-Nicene Fathers Volume 10. Grand Rapids, MI: Wm. B. Eerdmans Publishing, 1983.

GENERAL REFERENCE FOR BIBLE STUDY

Bianchi, Enzo. *Praying the Word: An Introduction to Lectio Divina*. Kalamazoo, MI: Cistercian Publications, 1998.

Browning, W. R. F (editor). *Oxford Dictionary of the Bible*. NY: Oxford University Press, 1996.

Hall, Thelma. *Too Deep for Words: Rediscovering Lectio Divina*. Mahwah, NJ: Paulist Press, 1988.

Johnson, Luke Timothy. *Living Jesus: Learning the Heart of the Gospel*. San Fransisco, CA: Harper Collins, 1999.

Manley, Johanna. *The Bible and the Holy Fathers*. Crestwood, NY: St. Vladimir's Seminary Press.

May, Herbert (editor). *Oxford Bible Atlas*. NY: Oxford University Press, 1985.

Metzger, Bruce (editor). *Oxford Guide to People and Places of the Bible*. NY: Oxford University Press, 2004.

Royster, Archbishop Dmitri. *The Kingdom of God: The Sermon on the Mount*. Crestwood, NY: St. Vladimir's Seminary Press, 1992.

_____. *The Miracles of Christ*. Crestwood, NY: St Vladimir's Seminary Press, 1999.

_____. *The Parables*. Crestwood, NY: St. Vladimir's Seminary Press, 1996.

Strong, James. *The New Strong's Exhaustive Concordance of the Bible*. Nashville, TN: Thomas Nelson Publishers, 1990.

Tarazi, Paul N. *The New Testament Introduction: Paul and Mark*. Crestwood, NY: St. Vladimir's Seminary Press, 1999.

_____. *The New Testament Introduction: Luke and Acts*. Crestwood, NY: St. Vladimir's Seminary Press, 2001.

ABOUT THE AUTHOR

Fr. William Mills, Ph.D., is the rector of the Nativity of the Holy Virgin Orthodox Church in Charlotte, NC, as well as an adjunct professor of religious studies at Queens University in Charlotte, NC. Fr. Mills received his Bachelor of History from Millersville University of Pennsylvania and then pursued theological studies at Saint Vladimir's Theological Orthodox Seminary in Crestwood, NY, where he received both Master of Divinity and Master of Theology degrees. He then pursued advanced theological studies at the Union Institute and University in Cincinnati, Ohio where he received his doctorate in Pastoral Theology.

Printed in the United States
62468LVS00005B/112-132

9 781933 275031

Prepare O Bethlehem is a collection of pastoral reflections on the Scripture readings that appear during the Christmas-Epiphany season. At Christmas, we prepare to once again receive Jesus into our lives, first as an infant, but also as our Lord, King and Savior. Ultimately, however, we receive him as the Word made flesh and we have "beheld his glory, glory as of the only Son from the Father." (John 1:14). This Word comes to us through the very words of scripture, for it is here, in the Old and New Testaments where we encounter the good news of our salvation. As we read through the scripture lessons for Christmas, Epiphany, and the Meeting of the Lord we are reminded that we are given the greatest gift of all, who is Jesus Christ himself. Unfortunately, the true "reason for the season" is often forgotten as we are bombarded by a myriad of holiday planning, parties, and activities that surround the holiday season. Hopefully we can take a few precious moments out of our busy schedules and patiently read the Word of God as we once again prepare to meet our Lord and Savior Jesus Christ, the Son of God.

FR. WILLIAM MILLS, PH.D., is the rector of the Nativity of the Holy Virgin Orthodox Church in Charlotte, NC, as well as an adjunct professor of religious studies at Queens University in Charlotte, NC. He is also the author of *From Pascha to Pentecost*.

ORTHODOX
RESEARCH
INSTITUTE

ISBN 1-933275-03-0

51395

9 781933 275031